Creating Your
ARCHITECTURAL STYLE

"Residential architecture is the index of the affluence of every civilization."

George Hopkins, Architect

Creating Your ARCHITECTURAL STYLE

DESIGNING AND BUILDING A FINE HOME

George D. Hopkins, Jr., Ph.D.
Architect

PELICAN PUBLISHING COMPANY

Gretna 2009

The word "Pelican" and the depiction of a pelican are trademarks
of Pelican Publishing Company, Inc., and are registered in the
U.S. Patent and Trademark Office.

ISBN 978-1-58980-719-8

Printed in China

Published by Pelican Publishing Company, Inc.
1000 Burmaster Street, Gretna, Louisiana 70053

This book is dedicated to my parents from whom I inherited my mother's determination and my father's ingenuity. Their love and steadfast support in the face of adversity helped me develop the confidence to pursue my dreams.

Contents

1300 block of First Street in the Garden District of New Orleans

Foreword

GEORGE HOPKINS AND THE AMERICAN HOME

Over a career spanning more than three decades, the New Orleans-based architect George Denègre Hopkins, Jr. has designed some 1,100 private homes from New York to Texas. Hopkins has indicated that since early childhood his sole ambition was to become an architect and design fine homes. Yet his professional route was not direct. Along the way he successfully advanced the concept of a major transportation corridor in New Orleans stretching from the Mississippi River Bridge to the Audubon Zoo. His doctoral dissertation at Tulane's School of Architecture focused on the adaptive reuse of historic buildings and touched upon everything from functionally obsolete warehouses to older housing stock in myriad styles.

In the end, Hopkins' direction evolved naturally from his own life. He was raised in the fabled Garden District, which remains to this day a living encyclopedia of American architectural styles in the nineteenth century. Even as a boy, Hopkins could admire the grand spaces, elegant proportions, and intriguing design elements of his family's home and those nearby. At the same time, he could readily see that those beautiful structures no longer accommodated the way people actually lived. Families had new interests and needs. Technology had opened new horizons. By the time he began his architectural studies, George Hopkins seemed to be facing a choice: either embrace the new and reject the rich heritage of style or adhere loyally to some classic prototypes and run the risk of turning into a dry antiquarian, out of touch with contemporary life.

Architects had been wrestling with this problem for more than a century, with all the polemics that seem to accompany debates within the profession. In Louisiana, in the 1960s and 70s both camps had distinguished representatives. Leading those who turned their backs on the traditional "styles" and focused instead on modernism was the firm of Curtis and Davis. In fact, Nathanial "Buster" Curtis was a next door neighbor of Hopkins and became a lifelong friend of the younger architect. Aligned on the side of traditionalism was the Baton Rouge-based architect A. Hays Town, who began a distinguished career designing private homes at age sixty. His meticulous evocations of classic Louisiana architecture dazzled the public and opened people's eyes to much that had been forgotten. Hopkins still reveres Town, just as he respects the achievements of the firm of Curtis and Davis. But in the end, he did not embrace either of their approaches. More precisely, he took what he found best in each, rejecting the rest; he then combined these and then added a third element of his own.

Through Buster Curtis he came to appreciate how a contemporary architect is able to translate the demands of modern life styles into comfortable and workable dwellings. Hays Town enabled him to appreciate the mastery that comes from a deep knowledge of the design elements of early styles. Hopkins concentrates on both sides of the equation, bringing to bear a social scientist's eagerness to identify and accommodate his clients' life styles and a virtuoso's knowledge of the major architectural styles to which Americans are drawn.

For George Hopkins, the choice of a style is not the beginning point for architecture and still less an end in itself. This selection can be made only when the patron has described the spaces to be included and their relative locations within the home. This may in turn be shaped by family composition, life style, ambition, available resources, or any combination of such factors. The results may be bland or wildly idiosyncratic, but the challenge is always the same: to translate real needs and wishes into practical functions and then to embody those functions in technologically up-to-date layouts and workable designs that are rendered coherent by a pleasing style.

Hopkins views the recent flood of American "McMansions" with a curious blend of disappointment and forbearance. Disappointment - because he sees that most designers of such dwellings have, at best, a sketchy knowledge of the elements of classic styles. Forbearance - because he knows how hard it is meet patrons' real needs while avoiding visual chaos. In the end, his approach recalls that of the great nineteenth century French Beaux Arts designers. Unlike some "purists," he gladly works in a variety of styles, approaches each with the respect it is due, and avoids mixing them. The breadth of Hopkins' palette of styles is the third element of his approach, and it derives both from his own broad sympathies and his patrons' diverse tastes.

Bluntly, then, the subject of this book is as much the men and women who set out to build a home for themselves as it is architecture per se. Clearly, the architect must bring to his task a keen knowledge of the cultural environment, social habits, and even the psychology of each of his patrons. This comes naturally to Hopkins. Quiet, but extremely observant, he has a novelist's ability to find the right pungent phrase to express what he hears or sees. At the same time, he has a rare capacity to empathize with his patron and help them express their feelings in terms of architecture.

This is a highly informative book, rich in uplifting insights, practical suggestions, and sober guidance. The splendid photographs, many of them by the architect himself, bring reality to the most arcane ideas and provide a kind of second text that amplifies and clarifies Hopkins' overall presentation. Here, then, is a book that enables the would-be home builder to understand his or her own wants and to come to grips with the endless issues that lurk along the winding path that leads from the initial impulse to their final realization in bricks and mortar.

One might be tempted to exclaim, "What an original idea!" But for all its innovations and insights, this book is by no means unprecedented. In fact, it occupies an honorable place in a great American tradition stretching from at least the 1830s to the present. The core of this tradition has been for architects to write books that help prosperous Americans express themselves through the design of their homes. Among the first to do this was New York-born Minard Lefever, who published no fewer than five "pattern books" between 1833 and 1850. However, Lafever addressed himself mainly to builders, not patrons. By contrast, Alexander Jackson Downing's books on Cottages and Residences (1844) and The Architecture of Country Houses (1850) were unabashedly intended to sidestep the architect and speak directly to the patron. They were hugely successful, as can be seen in the thousands of nineteenth century houses from coast to coast that were based on Downing's designs.

Other such books followed in quick succession. In 1851 Samuel Sloan, in Philadelphia, turned out two volume On Modern Architecture, which in turn inspired a Britisher, Calvert Vaux, to produce a widely read book, Villas and Cottages in 1857. Even as the Civil War was raging, one Henry Hudson Holly published Holly's Country Seats, presumably on the assumption that the war would end soon and prosperous Americans would return once more to the serious business of making homes for themselves.

Holly's book raises a question that is equally relevant to George Hopkins' book today: Is this endless concern for building homes for themselves a specific preoccupation of the rich? Why should anyone wish to perpetuate this tradition in a democratic age, especially when much of the world is mired in a deep economic slump? It is true that Vaux's extremely popular book on villas and cottages appeared just as the American economy was sinking under one of the first global financial panics, from which it fully emerged only with the outbreak of the Civil War, four years later. Not everyone who read Vaux's book could afford to build, but it helped thousands to crystallize their dreams of new ways to live that combined city and countryside, work and nature. Similarly, Holly encouraged his readers to dream at a time of national suffering. Who knows the extent to which such dreams, nurtured amidst extreme hardship, helped give rise to the enormous economic boom that blossomed after the surrender at Appomattox?

The desire to imagine for themselves an ideal home or residence is one of the constants of human civilization. It is reflected in the villas of ancient Romans, the palaces of Umayid caliphs, medieval fortresses, Renaissance palazzos, nineteenth century country estates, and the many residences that Frank Lloyd Wright designed for friends and neighbors in Oak Park and River Forest, Illinois. This desire seems particularly strong in democratic societies, and for an obvious reason. In democratic societies, as Alexis de Tocqueville noted, people fashion themselves, adopting ideals, values, and life styles on the basis of personal choice rather than tradition. The more prosperous the democracy, the more one might expect this basic urge to manifest itself.

And so we open this beautiful volume by George Hopkins. It can be leafed through, skimmed, read carefully but selectively, or pored over from beginning to end, with every approach rewarding the reader with understanding and pleasure. Those contemplating building a residence for themselves and their families will find countless practical tips herein. Those only dreaming of doing so will have their appetites whetted and their capacity for moving from dream to reality heightened. And those who have no desire at all to shackle themselves with a permanent residence of the sort discussed here, will take pleasure in the many intriguing insights Hopkins provides on the mores and values of the era in which we live.

S. Frederick Starr

Introduction

The complex process of planning and designing a new home is a daunting assignment for even the best-educated layperson. *Creating Your Architectural Style* levels the playing field and eliminates uncertainty about designing and building a new residence. Each chapter of this book is systematically organized to serve as both a framework for the planning process and a ready reference to resolve vexing issues. These insights will enable the reader to understand and orchestrate the task of designing and building a new home with the skill of an experienced project manager; acquire a complete understanding of the roles and responsibilities of each member of the design and construction team; gain the ability to describe the preferred design elements with the correct terminology; and identify the special features of your chosen architectural style or select the eclectic elements that combine to create your own personal style.

This book answers myriad questions posed by clients for whom we designed fine homes. Esoteric architectural terms and references to historical styles can be intimidating. Engineering components of the structural design and methods of construction are baffling. *Creating Your Architectural Style* addresses the division of responsibilities and sequencing of professional consultants including the architect, structural engineer, interior designer, landscape architect and a variety of specialists. Among these are kitchen planners, sound and video technicians, home theater designers, lighting consultants, security and special electronics experts.

There is an old expression, "They just don't build homes today as well as they used to." This is simply not true. Revolutionary advances in construction technology and upscale architectural design components are being incorporated into today's fine homes. Carefully engineered residences are being constructed that offer superior structural integrity with designs for sturdy foundations and framing to withstand storm force winds and other natural disasters. There have been remarkable accomplishments in interior environmental control, home automation, new materials requiring less maintenance and the development of every imaginable household fixture and appliance. Interest in the creative design of elegant homes is also stimulated by the Internet and monthly publications featuring exquisite photographs of magnificent residences built around the world. There are entire cable networks dedicated to residential design and building. *Creating Your Architectural Style* synthesizes and navigates a wealth of information to achieve all of your design objectives.

The key ingredients to the creation of a fabulous new home are time, talent and resources. This book will help you identify the roles and responsibilities of design team resources. It will also guide you through the construction process, helping to prevent costly mistakes and achieve superior results. If properly managed, creating your new home will be one of your most rewarding experiences. *Creating Your Architectural Style* will empower you to design your dream home as a reflection of your personal style.

During their travels to France, the owners of this manor house scoured the countryside for decorative design elements to embellish their new home. A guide led them to out-of-the-way warehouses from which they acquired gas lanterns, antique entrance doors, ironwork and furnishings. Even the casement windows are authentic, having been purchased from a French manufacturer.

Preferences for individual design elements are formed over a lifetime of aesthetic experiences. Thus, you have probably acquired or developed a personal inventory of design concepts and ideas that you wish to incorporate into your own special home. A client once expressed frustration at being unable to conceptually amalgamate the scores of ideas that she wanted to integrate into the layout for her new home. My response put her at ease by comparing the design requirements for her home to a 300-piece jigsaw puzzle piled in the middle of a table. Just as the first task with the puzzle is to sort the pieces of similar color, we must group spaces within a home into zones. The process for developing a floor plan is very similar to combining the partially assembled clusters of parts into the picture that appears when the puzzle is completed.

Over the past thirty-five years, it has been my professional responsibility to explain how to design fine homes to clients from a wide variety of geographic locations and to answer a multitude of questions on this subject. While each home that we design is uniquely tailored to our clients' individual needs and requirements, the process to achieve their architectural goals has been amazingly similar. *Creating Your Architectural Style* describes the basic issues that must be addressed when designing your home and how the parts of the puzzle fit together.

My confidence that this process will lead to a happy conclusion is reinforced by a casual, but telling, comment by another client whose home was under construction. As we were getting out of the car to inspect the newly framed walls, I asked if she would like for me to bring the plans. She said, "When we finished the drawings I could walk through this house in my sleep. I don't need the plans anymore because I know every inch of the layout." When we completed construction, she said that she wouldn't change a thing! This was certainly a rewarding measure of a successful design process.

The purpose of this book is to provide a thorough explanation of the process required to design fine homes. *Creating Your Architectural Style* is arranged in a fashion that will serve as a guide to organizing the approach to designing your home and as an informational resource defining architectural terms and describing residential styles.

Glistening at dusk, the porte-cochere and leaded glass doors illuminate the entrance to a new residence appointed with rusticated arches below a stone balustrade on the façade. Dormer windows open from guest suites on the second floor to a large front balcony.

Planning Your Style

Deciding to Build a New Home

The decision to build a new home generally follows an exhaustive search of houses for sale. While inspecting myriad existing residential properties, you will find many desirable features in the homes for sale. However, each of these houses will probably be disqualified for lack of one or more essential elements needed to satisfy your family's particular living requirements. At this point, you may wonder why you cannot find exactly the right home, in just the right neighborhood, in a real estate market comprised of so many homes that were planned for an equal number of families. With hundreds of different houses for sale in so many neighborhoods, one would think finding a home would be a relatively simple task. It is not and it never will be!

Every family that searches the existing housing market and fails to find the home of their dreams faces the same dilemma: will we compromise and purchase an existing residence that has some but not all of the features we really need, or should we build a new home that is creatively designed to include every special feature that we have always wanted?

The decision to purchase a building site and construct a new home does not come easily. Many families are afraid to approach a challenge as complex as building a new residence. There seem to be too many decisions, choices, expenses, risks, complications, potential frustrations and disappointments.

The old world charm of this spacious Mediterranean style home is accentuated by masonry stucco architectural details forming window and door cornices and rusticated arched openings emulating stone blocks that form the entry portico.

To properly satisfy your family's residential needs, you must be prepared to devote the time, attention and resources to create the design that precisely addresses your family's individual and collective needs and aesthetic preferences. Nobody else's dream house will do. No builder or existing home will achieve the combination of design elements that constitute your special home. Only by carefully integrating each of the design features that you have so thoughtfully identified can you enjoy the satisfaction of creating your own home.

When planning a new home, it is important to consider two elements of the design equation that distinguish different types of residential architecture — style and layout. First, your preference for a particular architectural style significantly limits the number of available residences that will satisfy your design requirements to a small percentage of the existing houses for sale. Secondly, your particular spatial needs require a carefully confected floor plan that addresses your family's lifestyle and individual hobbies, habits, recreational interests and leisure pursuits. These may include play spaces, entertaining areas, food preparation, eating and sleeping areas.

Left: Three dramatic arched openings are situated between the living room and wide center hallway of this 150 year old home. One arch is flanked by a pair of antique sconces with gold beaded shades.

Top Right: A skylight set in a stepped ceiling coffer provides a dramatic design element above the staircase in a Mediterranean style home.

Bottom Right: A pickled pine floor and tall double-hung windows covered with silk draperies provide the setting for a comfortable love seat and ottoman in the sitting room of a master bedroom suite.

The spatial needs for both large and small families are comprised of complex design requirements that must be skillfully planned to create an efficient and aesthetically pleasing arrangement of living spaces. Everyone requires creative solutions to meet their individual needs. Single professionals, families with grown children living at home, home-bound invalids and retired couples are a few examples of differing spatial needs for a new residence.

Thus, designing a new home is the opportunity of a lifetime to plan a residential environment that is custom tailored to your family needs and creatively designed to achieve your personal expression of aesthetic preferences.

Left: Views of the landscaped gardens from a brightly illuminated niche in the library create a tranquil spot to correspond.

Right: The design appointments and décor of the dining room offer a unique opportunity to express the owner's stylistic preferences ranging from architecture to interior design features. Each element of the design, from the shape of the room to the color of the walls and window treatments, contributes to the character of the dining environment.

Making Design Decisions

Making design decisions is often difficult for couples because husbands and wives usually have different perspectives. One memorable client meeting illustrates this dichotomy. Each spouse described the plan for the same house, but their priorities and concepts were completely different. It seemed impossible to incorporate both sets of ideas. Acknowledging the impasse, the husband turned to me and asked, "What do you do in a situation like this?" I am an architect, not a marriage counselor, so I responded respectfully: "I always side with the wife because she is ultimately going to prevail."

This anecdote does not imply that wives are more determined or uncompromising; nor should one infer that husbands don't have good ideas; and it does not mean that a wife's judgment is always correct. However, it has been my experience that a woman's judgment with respect to the home, daily routine and family needs is generally more insightful than her husband's.

Making design decisions with your spouse or partner requires the understanding that each partner is often interested in different aspects of the home. Since it is necessary to plan all aspects of the home, time and attention must be devoted to discussing the proposed layout, not only in general, but also in great detail.

Left: During their travels, the owners of this newly constructed Palladian style villa developed a deep appreciation for the characteristics of Italian architecture. They decided to purchase a riverfront site on a unique peninsula surrounded by the waters of the Bogue Falaya River. The design requirements for this site were similar to the residential structures they had admired in Venice. Rusticated arches on the ground floor frame views of the water from an open loggia and screened porch. Above at the main floor level, large arched windows in the living room face the river, flanked by iron balconies for the study and breakfast room. On the upper floor, the master bedroom is situated above the living room with an oculus window focused on the sky.

Right: The brightly illuminated master bedroom of this Italian style home features an oculus window below a barrel vaulted ceiling. Elegantly simple white draperies and furnishings enhance the airy feeling of this treetop bedroom suite.

Whether a family includes one or two working parents, the division of responsibility generally favors maternal coordination of the children's activities. Therefore, her familiarity with the children's study and play habits, bathing and dressing needs and the social compatibility among siblings provides valuable insights into the organizational structure that must be incorporated into the design of a new residence.

When it comes to design, it is my experience that women are often focused on the daily functional and operational necessities; while men tend to be primarily interested in the exterior style and leisure aspects of the home. Each family member has individual interests and habits that require particular accommodations. It is the combination of these special needs — and the space each requires — that makes the home you are planning different from all other houses. It is often these differences that require a design arrangement that is custom-tailored to your family needs.

The architect is responsible for guiding the owners through the process of making design decisions. This includes the drafting of a building program identifying all of the rooms that will comprise the home and how these spaces will be clustered together. The architect must create an artfully designed, functional layout in the form of floor plans and exterior elevations reflecting the owner's choice of architectural style.

So where do you begin? The first step is to develop a building program that describes the size and special features of each space in your new home. Since this is a written description rather than a layout, it really does not matter what you write down first. What is important is that you write down everything. Introducing a new element, like a second stair or an elevator, late in the design process can significantly alter the plans. Deciding to add or change design elements after beginning construction can be expensive, frustrating and delay the work.

The bright and airy design of this kitchen opens graciously to the yard and features French blue paneled cabinetry. Mexican limestone countertops and a beamed tongue and groove ceiling with pickled finish coordinate with the color of the tile floor.

The initial sequence for addressing design issues is flexible. If one partner is particularly concerned about planning a certain aspect of the home, tackle that issue first so that both can relax and participate with full concentration on planning the other areas of the home. Interestingly, when discussing a building program, each partner tends to identify the spaces he or she wishes to include in the home in the order of personal preference. Experience reveals that couples will often divulge their most pressing desires in order of priority during the first planning session.

It is important to listen attentively and note this information during the first discussion, eliminating the difficult task of trying to rank the owners' priorities from initial impressions. A keen understanding of the client's priorities will also help to identify the crucial design issues. This approach provides early detection of any conflicts couples may have in goals and desires for their home. Establishing consensus on the building program is fundamental to the development of a strong central concept, to which all subsequent design decisions must relate.

Having made these decisions about mutually established priorities, conceptual design, spatial requirements and a preferred architectural style, the building program is ready to be translated into schematic floor plans. Definite interrelationships between individual elements of the building must be established. This task involves zoning the interior spaces. Zoning involves grouping interior spaces into clusters, or zones, having dependent interrelationships. Each zone of the home is comprised of a group of spaces that function as a unit. For example, the master suite may include a large bedroom, bath area, dressing room, closets and perhaps a study or reading area that all combine to form one interior zone.

Top Left: The clean lines and sculptural massing of the beam ceiling and staircase of this contemporary kitchen create a handsome area for food preparation and casual dining.

Bottom Left: Antique pine ceiling beams in the solarium of a new plantation style home add to the timeless character of the design.

Top Right: The open plan of this vacation home in Watercolor is ideal for a casual lifestyle and entertaining friends and family on the Florida Gulf Coast.

Bottom Right: A wide porch wrapping around the façade overlooks a pond and lush greenery, providing a relaxing spot to read or converse.

Above: Adjoining the kitchen, a round table for six is the centerpiece of an informal dining area lit by two banks of triple windows.

Residential zones encompass particular uses and activities such as entertaining, cooking and dining, recreation, sleeping and personal privacy. A well-designed home includes a number of zones, each carefully configured and positioned with respect to other zones. The specific location of each zone within the home is determined by its function and special requirements for interaction with other zones. Together these zones form the floor plan that reflects, in diagrammatic form, the strong central concept developed from the building program.

Working in concert, the owners and architect should strive to create a cohesive architectural design that reflects a strong central concept. Through a cooperative effort and attention to detail, every design requirement must be addressed and thoughtfully integrated into the plans. Patience and persistence are required to thoroughly review and resolve each architectural issue, ensuring that the final design is pleasing to both partners.

Left: Linked to the main house, a solarium beside a swimming pool provides a secluded gathering place for family members and their friends.

Right: When viewed from the main house, a cabaña beside the swimming pool creates interest and a curious attraction that will draw your family and guests outside. The design of a cabāna often reflects the style and detailing of the main house or presents a whimsical contrast, depending on the design and layout of the grounds.

The Design Process

Developing a central design concept establishes the spine that links all of the residential zones of your home into a harmonious composition. Planning a new home involves the integration of many disparate design ideas into a strong central design concept. If the design process were viewed as a pyramid, the unifying concept would be at the top, flowing downward to the base. The hundreds of important, but subordinated, design elements form the base of the pyramid, combining to create the unique characteristics of your new home.

Unlocking the mystery of architectural design is a process that first involves identifying each of the spaces that will comprise your new home. This list of spatial requirements is called the building program and it documents all elements of the proposed new residence. These requirements include the size of rooms, shape, preferred views, intended use and stylistic design characteristics. The building program often identifies related design features such as cabinetry, millwork, flooring patterns and materials, fireplaces, ceiling designs, appliances and fixtures. Building programs may also include photographs depicting the preferred architectural style and illustrations of special features such as doors, windows, mantels, stairs and exterior design elements. Pictures from magazines are a great source of ideas for your design file. When you see an appealing picture, something attractive on the internet, or in a brochure, clip or save it in a file. It is never too soon to start a design file, even if you are just beginning to think about building a new home.

After listing all of the required spaces in your home, the next step is to organize the spaces into zones that identify rooms to be clustered near each other for convenience and function. An example of residential zoning is the relationship of the kitchen to the dining room, pantry and garage. These spaces are generally grouped in a zone to provide convenience for transporting groceries, preparing and serving meals and storing food, cookware and china.

Once a zone is defined, it is important to determine the position of each room within the zone and related design issues. For example, to provide a desired view from a window in the kitchen, the layout must

also consider relative positions of the dining room, pantry and garage that are interconnected within the same zone. Every family's priorities are different and the prominence of spaces for each home varies accordingly. Remember, every room is part of a zone; therefore, the layout must consider the design objectives of the most important room as well as its interrelationship with the accompanying spaces within the same zone.

Just as the individual rooms within a zone relate to each other, the group of zones that comprise your home must also coordinate in an organized fashion. It is this relationship that gives a home its functionality. While technical skill is needed to develop a workable spatial arrangement, architectural talent is required to transform a functional plan into an artistic composition, creating the design of a fine home.

The desire to create a new home that was truly authentic in style and materials prompted the owners of this Louisiana cottage to carefully select and store salvaged materials for use during construction. Antique pine from old warehouse buildings and sinker cypress from submerged logs were obtained from a variety of sources. The traditional lines of exterior design adhere to historical precedents. The bell shaped roof is accented by arched dormer windows with copper roofs. Tall double hung windows with operable shutters open directly from the main floor living areas onto a wrap-around porch overlooking a pond.

Your Lifestyle and Home Layout

Family lifestyles are shaped by unique combinations of individual characteristics and personal preferences. Each family member has a different lifestyle. Every member has an evolving pattern of active and passive activities. The interaction of these activities forms the family routine.

It is important that the layout of your home provide an arrangement of spaces to accommodate contemporaneous family activities. This is the lifestyle element of the design equation that adds individuality to the layout of your home. Each family member has special interests that must be addressed to fulfill his or her needs without conflicting with the activities of others.

Among the particular characteristics that shape your family lifestyle are age, gender, occupation, educational activities, physical attributes and limitations. Along with these fixed characteristics are individual interests that are equally influential but more variable. Typical examples are hobbies, sports, games, social activities and exercise routines. These are just a few of the personal interests and activities that combine to form the family lifestyle to be accommodated by the layout of your home. Another consideration is that these factors will change over time as each individual matures and your family progresses through life. This is why the spectrum of home design is so broad. One size, one style, cannot fit every family's needs.

The layout of this contemporary home is a reflection of the owner's casual lifestyle. An open floor plan allows rooms to flow graciously together and transcends the rigid framework that often divides a home into a series of separate spaces. Architectural elements such as the freestanding fireplace and large segmented arched openings define individual living areas without obstructing visual communication between spaces. As a result, everyone always feels a part of the ongoing activities.

Most family activities are part of a daily routine such as housekeeping, schoolwork, home office tasks and hobbies that recur on a regular schedule. Other activities occur only occasionally, such as special functions and home entertaining. In many cases, the observance of holidays or special events involves entertaining at home. These important elements of your family's lifestyle strongly influence the floor plan of your home.

The layout of your home must also respond to requirements for simultaneous activities that would be incompatible in the same or even adjacent spaces. It is difficult to listen to a television program over the sound of drum practice. The timing of different family activities determines the need for physical separation. The solution is a floor plan that eliminates incompatibility by providing physical or acoustical independence.

No family has a static lifestyle. The very nature of the family embodies growth and evolution. Careful thought about your family lifestyle, not only as it exists, but as it will evolve, is an important step in developing the criteria to be translated into the layout of your new home. The home that is designed to serve your family lifestyle now and for years to come is an enduring legacy, improving the quality of your life and that of each member of your family.

Left: This futuristic kitchen has come a long way from the basic function of food preparation and serving meals. Kitchen design often receives more time and attention than any other area of the home.

Right: The gentle breeze of a ceiling fan on a wide porch or lengthy veranda offers a soothing allure that many find irresistible. The ambiance of a graceful veranda, wrapping around the façade of a home, creates a timeless design element. The relaxing quality of an open porch provides a comfortable escape after a harried day.

Creating The Design

The Conceptual Design

What essentially distinguishes outstanding residential architecture from ordinary houses is the quality of the design concept that creatively unifies all of the elements of the home. To fully appreciate the value of a fine home, it is necessary to differentiate between the conceptual design and technical execution of the work.

An old adage is "no home is any better than its roof." Although this emphasizes the importance of watertight construction, it will only insure that your home will remain weatherproof. While the roof is certainly important, we have yet to design a new home where the first task was planning the roof details. This example may seem bizarre, but it illustrates that people with a penchant for technical details must be careful not to get swamped by the endless stream of product information about building materials, exterior finishes, doors, windows, flooring, mechanical systems, insulation, millwork, appliances and fixtures. It is a mistake to select all of the individual components and then try to assemble a house from a stockpile of unrelated parts.

Three separate component wings of a vacation home are linked by glass corridors and staggered to provide panoramic views of a lake surrounded by pine forest. The wing on the left is comprised of two guest suites. At the center, the main house has an open living area adjoining the kitchen and dining spaces. A loft bedroom with a dormer window is situated in the attic cavity above the kitchen. The right wing forms the master suite with a study-sitting area serving as an anteroom.

The design concept for a new home should be formulated from the top down, with all of the "details" as subordinated design elements. Conceptualizing the design should be approached from an overview rather than trying to resolve individual construction details or minor planning issues too early in the design process. It is practically impossible to create a great design without a unifying concept.

Developing the conceptual design for your new home is a creative endeavor involving the fundamental relationships of individual zones that comprise the architectural layout. Each zone constitutes a grouping of related areas that must be organized according to size, shape and relationship to other zones of the house. The creative arrangement of these zones significantly influences the composition of interior spaces and exterior shape of the house. Variations in the relationship of these zones will produce houses with distinctly different massing. It is important to recognize that residential massing, shape, size and scale will strongly influence the selection of a suitable architectural style for your home.

Left: A swimming pool becomes a reflecting pond, inverting the Neoclassical design of a riverfront home. Engaged pilasters beside arched openings supported by colonnettes define the loggia. Heavy stucco bracketed cornices above the upper floor windows of the main house coordinate with detailing of the Palladian windows on the side wings.

Right: Below the main roof, corbels on the broadly overhanging soffit add handsome detailing to the façade. Tall shuttered windows with stucco cornices provide access to an open porch with a classical balustrade above the main entrance. Hanging ferns and a landscaped brick walk create an intriguing pathway to the glowing white façade.

The key to developing the concept for your home is to determine the most pleasing massing and arrangement of internal zones that will create an exterior shape compatible with the form of the desired architectural style. A successful architectural design concept fully integrates the preferred layout and architectural style with the existing topography, sun orientation and landscape.

The central design concept is the fundamental theme that binds the zones of the home into a cohesive spatial arrangement fashioned with artistic ingenuity. The skill to design a fine home relies heavily on the ability to visualize compositions of solid geometry and create order out of an array of spatial requirements. This is the essence of architectural creativity. In some respects it is like tennis. There are great classic shots and unorthodox volleys. Experience and versatility generally rule the day. Designing a fine home is always challenging and exciting. Experienced residential architects specialize in addressing design problems and can help you avoid tedious or frustrating decisions.

Top Left: The symmetrical façade of a French Style home is delicately appointed with arches atop the portico, first floor windows, dormers and copper vents on the roof.

Bottom Left: French doors open from the three sides of the great room onto a wide colonnaded veranda overlooking the swimming pool, pavilion, gardens and greenhouse. Flagstone terraces graciously integrate outdoor living areas. The angular slate blue pool is long enough for swimming laps and contains an in-pool hot tub.

Top Right: A stately porte-cochère at the center of the façade provides a covered entrance to this French manor house that was designed to combine comfort and convenience with the ability to entertain large groups. All major living areas including the master suite are located on the ground floor with the exception of two upstairs guest suites, a morning kitchen and roof terrace.

Bottom Right: Inspired by the beautiful Greek Revival homes of New Orleans, time stands still when entering this stately new residence in southern Louisiana. Designed to the high standard of this renowned architectural style, every appointment of this home was crafted from the finest materials.

Selecting Your Architectural Style

Choosing the architectural style for the home you wish to build can influence the size, shape and layout of your house. This decision should not be made lightly, as its implications may be broader than you would expect. There are dozens of recognized architectural styles, each of which is distinguished by its design elements, shape and scale.

In my experience, men and women often have different priorities when designing a new home. Men generally seem to be more interested in the exterior appearance of the house, while women usually focus more on the interior design. This is not meant to imply that either party isn't interested in other aspects of the design. It simply illustrates that priorities often differ when two people embark on a home planning process.

The selection of an appropriate architectural style requires the contemporaneous analysis of interior and exterior design objectives to achieve a compatible stylistic approach. Individual preferences for architectural styles are derived from many sources. Some choose an architectural style based on an affinity for a former home or another house they have always admired. Others desire to make an architectural statement or have an interest in pursuing a particular lifestyle. Whatever the motivation, proper styling is an essential element of every successful residential design.

Two-story Ionic columns support the stately curved portico of an Italian villa-style residence in Alabama. A terra cotta tile roof coordinates with the old brick walkway, steps and porch floor at the main entrance. Stucco exterior with banding at the floor levels and a wide, horizontally proportioned triple pane dormer are characteristically Italian features.

The selection of an architectural style helps define the shape and features that will combine to form the interior and exterior design of your home. These include the types of windows and doors, roof, porches and special features that will create the visual image of your house. These architectural elements, especially the style of openings in the exterior walls, will also be reflected on the interior walls. This means that windows and doors must simultaneously satisfy design requirements for the exterior style and interior decor. To avoid painful design changes later, make certain that windows and doors of the selected architectural style are compatible with the preferred interior decor. This may seem obvious, but it is often overlooked.

Residential design priorities may vary with respect to decisions about the exterior style versus the layout of the interior floor plan. Simply put, some houses are designed from the outside in, while other homes are planned from the inside out. The approach depends upon your priorities. However, the decision to independently pursue one without consideration of the other usually results in problems with the design.

If you design from the outside in, the scale and proportion of the spaces within the home will be strongly influenced by the exterior massing and fenestration of the chosen architectural style. Conversely, if your home is fundamentally designed from the inside out, the floor plan may result in a layout that will not accommodate the preferred exterior style. Whether you start designing the layout for your new home from the inside or from the outside, ultimately the two must be a geometrically compatible marriage of the architectural style and floor plan.

Top Left: A country residence is elevated on brick piers to provide a ground floor workshop and parking for cars and boats. Main Floor living areas open to a wrap-around porch with expansive views of the surrounding fields.

Middle Left: A classic cottage is flanked by side wings housing the master suite and a three car garage. The children's bedrooms are upstairs above the living areas at the center of the house.

Bottom Left: Situated by a pond in Westchester County, this two-story wood frame home is bisected by a long central stairhall. The living room, to the right of the hallway, and an enclosed solarium extend completely through the home providing views of the front lawn and hillside behind the house.

Top Right: Situated at the bend in a wide river, this French style residence emulates the charming chateaux of the Loire Valley.

Bottom Right: The Italian influence on the design of this home is reflected in the arched portico, symmetrical façade and refined exterior fenestration.

Other issues that must be addressed when selecting an architectural style are suitability, compatibility and cost. Nearly every region of the world has an indigenous architectural style. Each regional style is responsive to its environment including accommodations for seasonal variations in temperature, rainfall, snowfall, flood elevation, hurricane protection, natural ventilation and shade from the sun. When choosing an architectural style, these environmental factors should be considered so that the selected style will be well-suited to your region. This ensures comfort and convenience while providing durability and weatherproofing that add longevity to the structure.

If the characteristics of your preferred architectural style are appropriate for the region's environment, consideration should also be given to design compatibility within the neighborhood. The smaller the building site, the closer together homes are constructed. Therefore, the "tout ensemble" or collective appearance of all homes becomes important. On larger building sites where homes are further apart, the design relationship between adjacent homes is less significant.

The choice of an architectural style can strongly influence the project budget. Certain styles require expensive slate or tile roofs, while others feature costly millwork, galleries or ornamentation. A better understanding of the cost of special design elements at the outset of the project can avoid shock or disappointment when negotiating with contractors. Remember, a delicate balance must be struck between quality and quantity. A small, handsomely appointed home can cost just as much as a large house constructed entirely of stock building components.

Modeled after the majestic Neoclassical plantation homes along the Mississippi River, this new residence is zoned internally to provide a private master suite in the right side wing linked to the main house by a sitting room. On the left side, a garage and attic playroom are connected to the main house by the kitchen and breakfast room. Children's bedrooms are located on the second floor, above the great room, library and dining room. Rooftop dormer windows illuminate living spaces in the large attic.

In the end, the most important test for suitability of architectural style is its compatibility with the floor plan. There is an inextricable relationship between the architectural style and floor plan of your home. To create a successful residential design, the external shape and massing of the chosen style must fit the layout of the interior spaces. More particularly, the relationship among the various zones of the house, as organized in the conceptual design, defines the mass of the home. When the interior layout is subordinated to the exterior style, compromises are often required in the design of rooms. Alternatively, when the floor plan is given priority, the desired exterior style may be compromised. In either case, the design typically requires a series of refinements to the interior spaces and exterior appearance to achieve compatibility between architectural style and layout.

Top Left: Gracious living areas of this French style residence occupy the ground floor of the main house with children's bedrooms in the attic above. A master suite and guest quarters are located in the left wing and a breezeway links the main house to the garage.

Bottom Left: A handsomely appointed Federal-style home features limestone quoins on the corners of the façade with a main entrance flanked by pairs of engaged columns below and arched pediment. A classical circular window is situated above on the second floor beneath the triangular roof pediment with details in bas-relief.

Top Right: A breezeway links the main house to the garage of a country cottage with side wings. The kitchen is conveniently located in the left side wing with the breezeway creating a side entrance for family and friends. The master suite is on the right side of the house. Three dormer windows in the main roof provide light and ventilation for children's bedrooms upstairs.

Middle Right: Perched on a sandy berm overlooking the marsh at Amelia Island, a raised cottage featuring an open porch on the façade and matching screen porch on the marsh side.

Bottom Right: Nestled on a prominent site in the Garden District of New Orleans, the design of this recently constructed Georgian brick cottage incorporates classic architectural appointments into a carefully confected floor plan that addresses the owner's desire for graciously flowing interior entertaining areas.

Relating the Style and the Floor Plan

The relationship between the architectural style and the floor plan for your home is the marriage of its shape and mass to the arrangement of spaces. When choosing an architectural style, it is essential to further explore how the stylistic design of the exterior will affect the interior composition of your new home. Compatibility of these elements is vital to the development of a strong design concept. The following examples illustrate design issues that arise when endeavoring to achieve interior and exterior design compatibility.

A typical two-story Colonial home in New England often consists of two rectangular floors that are identical in size and shape. This style of home would be difficult to accomplish if the owner wanted the majority of the interior spaces to be on the first floor including the master bedroom suite, kitchen, great room, dining room, family room, study, foyer and garage. The remaining spaces to be located on the second floor would be limited to a few bedrooms and bathrooms. Obviously, the area requirements for the ground floor are much greater than the second floor. It is impossible to design a viable layout for a home with two identical floors when the area requirements for each floor differ significantly. This spatial distribution and internal zoning arrangement would be better suited to a different style, perhaps a one-and-a-half story Acadian style cottage having only two or three bedrooms in the attic.

Achieving the proper massing to produce the preferred architectural style requires artfully assembling entire zones of the home into an arrangement that marries the interior plan with the external shape. Inside, the optimum layout and circulation must function while establishing the appropriate exterior mass to achieve the design of the selected style.

Reminiscent of the stately homes along St. Charles Avenue in New Orleans, this Italianate residence was designed for comfortable family living surrounded by lush gardens and greenery. A classic stone balustrade on the second floor balcony is supported by Ionic columns elegantly forming the entry portico.

As an example, Georgian façades typically include a central front door with a feature window directly above at the second floor level. Two or three double-hung windows generally flank the entrance to form a symmetrically balanced façade. Windows on the first and second floors are always aligned vertically. The façade of a Georgian style home strongly influences the layout of interior rooms. A foyer is usually situated directly behind the front entrance at the center of the house. The living and dining rooms often open to opposite sides of the foyer, each having matching symmetrically-placed façade windows. The second floor of a Georgian style plan reflects the exterior massing of the house. The layout usually includes bedrooms at both front corners with vertically aligned windows above the living and dining rooms.

This illustration underscores the important relationship between architectural style and interior layout. If style takes precedence, the façade of your home will strongly influence the layout. Conversely, if the interior floor plans are developed without considering the exterior implications, your choice of architectural styles may be limited.

Top Left: A bold arched entry portico is the focal point at the center of a symmetrical French façade. Segmented arches on the tall ground floor windows are reflected in the design of dormer windows on the roof.

Bottom Left: A wrap-around veranda continues on three sides of the main house supported by clusters of Doric columns. A bay-shaped sun room and library on the left side open to a flagstone porch with steps to the yard. In the background, a two-story carriage house provides parking for three cars and a cabaña bath on the ground floor. Upstairs, a guest suite, artist studio and sun deck face the swimming pool.

Top Right: Limestone trim below the eaves and surrounding windows and doors embellish the classic design of this stately home.

Middle Right: Raised on a brick base for protection against flooding, the main floor of this West Indies style home is nestled in a tropical landscape reminiscent of the islands.

Bottom Right: This classic contemporary home is similar in mass to the top photo, but distinctly different in floor plan and styling. The arrangement of interior spaces is inverted, positioning living spaces and the master suite on the upper level to allow for vaulted ceilings and capture panoramic views. Children's bedrooms, a playroom and garage are located below on the ground floor.

Whether you choose to design your home from the inside out or the outside in, the interior and exterior configurations must be geometrically compatible. A truly successful residential design fully integrates the architectural style and floor plan in the early stages of conceptual design.

These two homes illustrate the variation in urban and rural approaches to residential design. The West Indies style home (below) opens to an elegant flagstone courtyard. The country home (right) has a veranda overlooking clusters of live oak trees and open fields beyond the shell driveway.

Architectural Styles

Overview of American Styles

American residential architecture is a fascinating collection of styles born of necessity, borrowed from native homelands, or based on classical design principles. Indigenous housing types, including the simple and practical Saltbox and Cape Cod homes, were constructed of available building materials and designed to endure the northeastern climate. European residential concepts were transplanted to the new world and classical design principles were applied to the design of fine homes and buildings. Early Colonial architecture, from its beginning in Jamestown, reflected the European design characteristics of English, Spanish, Dutch and French homes.

The residential styles presented in this section address the architectural design characteristics of many outstanding homes built in America. Particular emphasis has been placed on those styles that continue to influence the design of new residences. The evolution of trends in American architectural style often reflect political circumstances, wars, economic prosperity and the cultural heritage of the settlers. Diversity of cultural origins manifested itself in a broad spectrum of architectural expression. A prosperous agrarian nation, that subsequently became industrialized, created an opportunity for the construction of magnificent homes in a remarkable array of architectural styles.

In many cases, American residential architecture is classified by reference to the historical styles of Europe. For instance, the Georgian style was imported by English settlers in the 1700s. Georgian architecture flourished in the colonies until the Revolutionary War when it evolved into the Federal style after the war destroyed relations with England. The Georgian style lay dormant for a hundred years after the revolution until the American centennial celebration created a nostalgic return to the Georgian residential style. The Federal style continued in popularity as an American adaptation of Georgian architecture.

West Indies-style homes began to appear in the South circa 1750 as an American architectural expression of the island sugar plantations. Trading relationships between New Orleans and the West Indies developed a cultural exchange. Some traders who traveled to the islands returned and constructed large homes emulating the simple West Indies residential designs with modest ornamentation. Similarities in climate made the West Indies style very adaptable to the warm, rainy weather of the South. Wide galleries provided comfortable outdoor living and allowed cross ventilation through open windows.

The Greek Revival style emerged contemporaneously with Federal architecture after the revolutionary war. For the next seventy years many important public and private buildings were constructed throughout the country in the Greek Revival style. From a political standpoint, the Greek Revival style became a symbol of the American democratic form of government. Its ancient rules of classic order and proportions also strongly influenced the design of many prominent Southern plantation homes built in the mid-1800s before the Civil War.

Initially, Southern plantation homes were simply designed and modestly detailed, reflecting basic colonial resources. However, as agriculture along the Mississippi River prospered, the scale, style and ornamental detailing of these homes evolved into massive, refined and elaborate edifices. Plantation homes were usually situated on large crop farms and were grander in scale than houses in town. While designed for functionality, these homes were usually formal in nature. Southern plantations were designed in a variety of architectural styles including Georgian, West Indies, French Colonial, Eclectic and the classical Greek Revival.

In the mid-1800s, Italian architecture gained prominence in America and was especially popular in major growth areas extending across the United States from the northeast to California. These stucco or stone homes were also easily identifiable by distinctly Italian design elements such as a belvedere or campanile, large brackets supporting wide overhangs, heavy cornices and low-pitched tile roofs.

Contemporaneously with the proliferation of Italian architecture in America, the Victorian era produced a variety of outstanding architectural styles that also became exceptionally popular. Among these styles were the ornamental and colorful Queen Anne homes distinguished by their woodwork details, asymmetrical shape, wrap-around porches, turrets, towers, and steeply pitched roofs. Although less prevalent, Eastlake Victorian preceded the Queen Anne style with even more elaborate detailing. Other forms of Victorian architecture include the Gothic Revival, Italianate, Richardson Romanesque and Second Empire styles.

The French residential style became popular in the United States after World War I when American forces returned home with an appreciation for French architecture. French architectural characteristics from the regions of Normandy and Brittany were transformed into an eclectic American interpretation of this informal, asymmetrical style with steep hipped roofs and dormer windows to light and ventilate attic rooms.

Mediterranean-style homes became popular in America after the Great Depression. These homes were similar to their European counterparts built along the Italian seacoast. Eclectic adaptations of this style are prevalent today in Florida, California and coastal areas of the Gulf of Mexico.

The Neoclassical style originated during the Italian Renaissance with the work of Andrea Palladio. The term Neoclassical architecture indicates a revival of ancient Greek and Roman design principles. Homes and buildings of this style are comprised of classical design elements and employ the associated rules of scale and proportion. In Scotland and England, architects Robert and James Adam subsequently introduced the Neoclassical style during the 1700s. In America, at the turn of the 20th century, the firm of McKim, Mead and White designed many prominent Neoclassical homes and public buildings. The U.S. Capitol and Supreme Court Building are among the most prominent Neoclassical buildings in Washington. Outstanding examples of Neoclassical residences include Thomas Jefferson's home, Monticello, the White House and many of the impressive Southern Plantation mansions

Modern architecture of the early 20th century broke with the past and abandoned historical styles for severity and simplicity. The International style dominated the design of high rise buildings creating austere rectilinear structures with glass curtain walls, flat roofs, and modular façades. Prominent architects of this period included Walter Gropius, LeCorbusier, and Mies van der Rohe. Modern architecture had more influence on office buildings than residential design. In contrast to the institutional austerity of the International style, Frank Lloyd Wright developed an organic context for a number of remarkable residences in the early 1900s that were uniquely his own creation. Often called the Prairie Style because of their low, horizontal lines, these homes almost appear to grow out of the ground.

The term Contemporary architecture describes the current period of design expression that covers a broad spectrum of stylistic approaches. Design styles presently classified as Contemporary include brutalism (bare concrete structures), post-modern (a rejection of the International style), deconstructivism (distorted shapes), high-tech (industrial) and classic contemporary (traditional forms/contemporary detailing). Prominent architects of this period are Paul Rudolph, Louis Kahn, Robert Venturi, Peter Eisenman, Michael Graves, Charles Moore, and Frank Gehry.

Residential architecture in America presently reflects the influence of post-World War II prosperity. This era has fostered an amazing transition from modest suburban homes built for the families of returning servicemen to the extravagant and opulent upscale residences of recent design. Ceiling height alone is a remarkable index of the times. The standard eight foot interior height of 1950s and 1960s ranch style homes gave way to nine foot ceilings in the 1970s. By the 1980s, the upscale residential ceiling height was ten feet and in the 1990s a select group of major residences were built with twelve foot ceilings that were the standard in many Southern homes before the Great Depression.

Concurrent with post-war prosperity, a proliferation of books and periodical publications featuring upscale residential architecture and interior design have captured the imagination of almost anyone interested in building a new home. Each month, popular residential styles are prominently featured in settings ranging from major cities to mountains and tropical islands.

After repeated exposure to a diversity of architectural styles and an even greater collection of magazine photographs, choosing a residential style for a new home can become overwhelming. If this is not enough to boggle one's mind, trying to integrate stylistic preferences with a workable floor plan while simultaneously capturing your favorite exterior design can seem like an impossible task.

Purely historical architectural styles rarely satisfy all of the particular needs of a contemporary lifestyle. Addressing the unique requirements of each family member often requires an eclectic design solution created within the framework of a preferred architectural style, especially in terms of the residential layout and interior finishes.

Understanding the elements of historical styles is the foundation for creating your style. This chapter is designed to provide an overview of residential architectural styles in America. It will be helpful in determining your personal preferences for the style of your new home.

Colonial Architecture

(1607-1780)

During the 17th century, thousands of settlers left England and various parts of Europe to cross the Atlantic and colonize the New World. In 1607, the English settlement at Jamestown spawned an adaptation of residential architecture rooted in European historical styles and building traditions. The diverse cultural influences of these early settlers formed America's Colonial architecture from 1600-1780.

Because of the scarcity of conventional building materials in the colonies, older European residential designs had to be modified. Weather conditions in America were harsh compared to the milder European climate, also necessitating changes in design. For example, steep English roofs were replaced by lower-pitched ones because thatched roofing material performed poorly on homes in the New World. Split shingles, or "shakes," replaced thatched roofs because they could shed water from a lower-pitched roof.

The term "Colonial," when it is expressed without a specific national reference, generally refers to English Colonial architecture. However, Colonial architecture can also be more specifically classified by the terms "French, Spanish, Dutch and English" when referring to the imported design characteristics from these countries. Each Colonial architecture type derives its characteristics from its heritage. For instance, thick adobe brick walls and low-pitched or flat roofs usually reflect Spanish Colonial architecture, while French Colonial houses are generally timber framed with high-pitched roofs.

Colonial architecture eventually lost popularity for political reasons during the American Revolution because of the conflict with England. This residential style diminished in construction until the late 1800s and early 1900s, when there was a rebirth of interest in English and Dutch Colonial styles.

French Colonial

(1700-1830)

The French controlled an immense North American territory in the 18th century. However, few examples of the French architecture from this period have survived. Construction of French Colonial homes diminished after the Louisiana Purchase in 1803, except in New Orleans. As a result, French Colonial architecture has had little influence on subsequent residential architectural design. Surviving examples of this style are located along the Mississippi River south of St. Louis, and throughout Louisiana, especially in New Orleans.

Urban and rural building traditions in the French Colonial style were quite different. The remaining urban French Colonial homes in New Orleans are one-story row houses constructed at ground level and raised galleried houses. Rural French Colonial residential construction differs from its urban counterpart because its main floor is usually being built high above the ground on masonry foundations to protect the home from flooding. Galleries usually surround the home with rows of thin wooden columns supporting the lower slope of the roof. Rural French Colonial homes are generally much larger than houses of the same style built in the city.

French Colonial homes often consist of two stories. These houses rarely have hallways since each room typically has a doorway to the outside or opens directly into another room. Stairs are usually on the outside of the building. Outside staircases and the absence of interior hallways make porches or galleries essential features of the French Colonial home. The overhanging gallery at the second floor level, enclosed by a simple balustrade running between the columns, creates a corresponding covered porch on the ground floor. Massive porches often surround the entire structure and provide the only means of circulation from room to room. Galleries are prominent elements of the French Colonial home and often feature decorative posts.

Early French Colonial homes had steeply pitched roofs similar to English and Dutch Colonial structures. This design typically followed the medieval tradition of providing a steep pitch to shed water from thatched roofs. Subsequent French Colonial homes featured large hipped roofs sheltering the interior living quarters with a lower-pitched roof extending over the gallery. This technique originated in the West Indies and was frequently employed by the French Colonial settlers and their descendants who built the more elaborate plantations. Variations of stucco materials were used to finish both interior and exterior walls. Wood from the region, particularly cypress, was used for posts and beams.

French Colonial houses always utilized batten shutters rather than the louvered shutters that were common on later southern houses. These shutters could be simple designs or decoratively paneled, depending on the formality of the house.

French doors are a distinct characteristic of this Colonial style. These door openings are similar in width to a conventional door; however, individual leafs of the door are narrower because it is divided in half vertically to create two smaller doors within one frame. This French style double door has remained popular and is commonly used today. Like the French doors, French Colonial windows have the same vertical division and operate as casements rather than sliding open vertically.

The lower half of French Colonial double doors often includes a panel. Glass was only used above the middle rail and the panes were stacked vertically in a group of four or five panes. French windows usually match the doors giving the home unified design. Decorative moldings around the windows and doors of a French Colonial home were generally more elaborate than other Colonial styles.

English Colonial

(1600-1780)

The English Colonial houses built following the initial settlement of North America were generally late medieval structures. Early structures built in America by the British became known as "Post-Medieval" English houses. This was the only architectural style built in the colonies until around 1700 when Georgian architecture was first introduced. The major characteristic that dintinguishes "Post-Medieval" English Colonial houses from Georgian homes is a lack of ornamentation. The early English Colonial house was primarily functional with little attention to decoration.

In plan, early English Colonial homes were typically symmetrical and one room deep. Later, lean-to additions were integrated into the plan and the familiar "saltbox" residence having a double-pitched rear roof was developed. In the northern colonies, timber framing was covered with wood shingles to form walls on two-story houses. Most houses in the southern colonies were typically one-story buildings of either timber framing or brick construction. English Colonial houses were rarely painted, usually remaining unfinished or covered with a coat of oil.

The design of English Colonial homes included large chimneys made of solid masonry that were either centrally located or situated at one end of the building. Windows of early homes were small and comprised of diamond-shaped glass panes that were fixed in place. Eventually builders developed operable window sashes. The cornice or eave below the roof was usually plain without design details. The front door of the English Colonial home was composed of vertically joined wooden boards with little or no decoration. Decorative moldings were rarely used on windows and doors and only a simple sill and trim board surrounded these openings.

The English Colonial style of American architecture has remained popular because of its adaptability in plan and classic simplicity in design. The symmetry of the façade, scale and proportions of the English Colonial home provide a timeless aesthetic quality that continues to garner broad general appeal.

Dutch Colonial

(1614-1800)

Though Dutch control of the colonies in the New World was very brief, it significantly impacted the design of houses built at the time. Urban Dutch Colonial houses in America are similar to their European counterparts. Early American examples of this architectural style displayed European features including simple masonry walls of stone and gable roofs. These residential structures later acquired unique characteristics that are distinctly associated with Dutch Colonial architecture.

The gambrel roof is the most uniquely Dutch feature of this style of colonial residence. This uniquely shaped roof has four sides making it appear tall. The eaves often flare at the bottom and deeply overhang the rest of the structure. The gambrel roof facilitated long roof spans and enhanced usable attic space within the home. Gambrel roofs were built more often in the countryside than in urbanized areas. Dutch Colonial towns were often comprised of buildings with simple gabled roofs and heavy stone end walls extending above the roofline to form parapets at either end of the building and incorporating two massive chimneys.

Dutch Colonial houses were built in a rambling style as new living spaces were needed. When the original home was outgrown, a larger version was erected immediately adjacent to the old structure that functioned in an ancillary capacity to the new enlarged home. Other living spaces were subsequently added to the house as needed.

The original Dutch Colonial residences featured double hung windows with two levels of glass stacked one above the other. Windows and doors were fashioned in wood, often with simple lintels and sills. Shuttered windows and doors were sometimes featured on the façade.

Doors were constructed of simple wood slats, arranged vertically with very little or no detailing. Occasionally, exterior doors of a Dutch Colonial-style house were divided horizontally into upper and lower panels that would open separately. This would allow fresh air to enter the home while keeping farm animals out.

Common features of the Dutch Colonial style have become an integral part of American architecture. The Dutch gambrel roof design frequently appears in rural areas above a barn to increase the volume of a hay loft. One modern legacy from this vintage style is the Dutch door that is widely used for pass-through convenience in commercial establishments. For generations, Dutch design elements from the colonial period have been assimilated into American residential design.

Spanish Colonial and Revival Styles

(1600s-1940)

The Spanish came to the New World in the 1600s to conquer and rule various regions and convert the natives to Christianity. They subsequently founded missions in Florida, Texas, California, New Mexico and Arizona. Indigenous materials were used to build Spanish Colonial-style homes because the regions where they were constructed were isolated and impoverished. These homes had to be simple and inexpensive, so adobe brick or stone was used to build the walls. These homes were usually one-story structures comprised of massive, uniquely curved masonry walls and a flat or low-pitched roof. Examples of Southwestern adobe architecture dating back to the 17th century are still standing today, demonstrating its long-lasting durability.

Spanish Colonial houses possessed very little ornamentation or articulation of design features until 1830 when open trading in the United States increased the affluence of these areas. Spanish Colonial homes often included a narrow porch that ran along the interior courtyard of the structure. As with French Colonial houses, the porches provided the only means of access to each room. The rambling forms of these homes were the result of constructing various rooms as they were needed. A small dwelling was initially constructed and, when more space was needed, other rooms were added to the original structure.

The Spanish architecture of Central and South America has made an indelible impression on the design of houses in the western United States. In the late 19th century, a renewed interest in local Spanish and Mexican architecture began in southern California. Aptly dubbed the Mission Revival style, the early Spanish missions inspired this architectural style. The Mission Revival style spread to other parts of the United States after the turn of the 20th century. Typical features include a red tile roof and stucco walls, serpentine parapet walls and mock bell towers reminiscent of the 17th and 18th century missions.

About the same period, the Pueblo Revival style gained popularity. It sought to imitate the traditional adobe structures of the pueblos and Spanish missions in New Mexico. Homes of the Pueblo Revival style were constructed of adobe or modern materials that simulated adobe. Unique attributes of the Pueblo Revival style include stepped massing between floor levels and non-structural wooden beams projecting below the eave of the roof.

Following the Panama-California Exposition in 1915, the Spanish Colonial Revival style gained widespread attention. Although this style appeared most prominently in the former Spanish colonies of Texas, Florida, California and Arizona, it eventually spread throughout the country. The Spanish Colonial Revival is distinguished from the Mission and Pueblo styles because its design elements are derived directly from Spain, rather than incorporating Mexican features. However, shared characteristics with the Mission style include low-pitched tile roofs with little or no overhang and an asymmetrical smooth stucco exterior. The Colonial Revival style generally excludes curved parapets and towers.

Colonial Revival is the most decorative of the Spanish styles. Colonial Revival homes often include a second story with recessed porches and balconies, spiral columns, carved stonework or pilasters and arches over paired or triple windows. Other features of this style are decorative ironwork, interior courtyards, patios, fountains, dentil moldings and certain Greek Revival details.

New homes constructed in the Spanish Colonial style incorporate many of the traditional adobe design elements including low-pitched or flat roofs that are best suited to the dry or semi-desert climate of the Southwest. However, the exterior walls of new homes are generally constructed of a mixture of cement and plaster that is hand troweled on insulated wood or metal framing that is covered with wire mesh instead of building thick adobe walls.

Colonial Revival

(1880-1955)

After the American Revolution in 1776, Colonial architecture fell out of favor with architects and builders. The construction of homes in this style came to a sudden halt. Many Americans were not interested in building anything associated with their colonial past. New homes were designed in a style intended to reflect the vast wealth and success of American entrepreneurs who considered the humble style of Colonial architecture inappropriate. This approach dominated residential construction in America for the next hundred years. However, after the American Centennial celebration of Independence in 1876, people become nostalgic for the Colonial style.

The Centennial Exposition in Philadelphia inspired a revival of the Colonial style leading to its domination over other architectural styles of the time. Although the Colonial Revival typically refers to the rebirth of interest in the English and Dutch Colonial styles, the Georgian and the Federal styles of residential architecture were also major components of this revival period. Colonial Revival homes are not usually pure reproductions of Colonial houses, but tend to be combinations of Georgian, Federal and Colonial styles.

Houses built in the Colonial Revival style are easily distinguished from the original Colonial architecture because they were seldomly reproduced accurately. For example, many Colonial Revival-style houses have paired windows that do not appear in the design of original Colonial homes. Colonial Revival houses also tend to have more detailed ornamentation, while the original Colonial homes were generally simple. Before 1910, the two designs that characterized the Colonial Revival style were the asymmetrical shape with colonial ornamentation and the traditional symmetrical hipped roof configuration.

The façades of Colonial Revival homes are usually flat and symmetrical. Classical ornamentation such as decorative cornices and classically ordered columns are frequently used in moderation on Colonial Revival homes. Colonial Revival homes typically have gabled, hipped, or gambrel roofs. Dormer windows are sometimes included to provide habitable attic space.

Colonial Revival houses, like Federal style, often feature a small pedimented portico supported by columns or pilasters to enhance the main entrance. Unlike the original English Colonial style, Colonial Revival homes often have pairs or even triple windows on the façade. The front door is commonly paneled and decorative with a transom and side lights frequently adjacent to the door. Exterior shutters are a common feature on Colonial Revival windows.

Today, Colonial Revival homes are present in many older developments built in the United States. These homes were easy to construct and affordable during a period of rapid expansion of the housing market. Myriad versions of the Colonial Revival home have since been constructed by speculative builders assembling Colonial design elements in an eclectic manner. These homes are unique interpretations of the original Colonial architecture.

Georgian Architecture

(ca. 1700-1875)

In response to the ostentatious opulence of the Baroque style, European architecture became reserved and dignified. Georgian homes in England were designed in this classical tradition and served as a model for the Georgian style in America. As a result of this British influence, the Georgian style became the most prevalent form of residential architecture constructed in the English colonies in the 18th century.

The Georgian style of architecture was inspired by the designs of the Italian Renaissance architect Andrea Palladio. The simple elegance and formality of Palladian designs, exhibiting the classic principles of geometric proportion and symmetry, became the essence of the Georgian style. One of the finest examples of Georgian architecture reflecting the Palladian influence is Drayton Hall built in South Carolina (1738-42). An equally significant Georgian mansion, Carter's Grove, was constructed in Virginia during the 1750s.

Georgian architecture also adopted a less dramatic scale and certain design elements from Dutch residential architecture of the late 17th century. These features included brickwork with contrasting details in sandstone and hipped roofs. A pedimented portico was often placed at the center of the Georgian façade above the main entrance. Domes were sometimes employed to emphasize the volume of major interior spaces. Georgian style residences are generally comprised of two stories with a tall, steep-pitched roof covering the house. However, one-story Georgian homes are occasionally built.

Georgian façades are almost always perfectly symmetrical. The Georgian roof is often decorated with dormer windows and may also include a balustrade running along the ridge of the roof. Ornamentation on Georgian style homes is usually sparse and restricted to the decorative features surrounding the doors and windows. A cornice with decorative moldings or dentils is situated below the eave of the roof to embellish the façade at the soffit. These design elements combine to offer residential architecture a sense of classic elegance.

The Georgian front door is typically centered on the principal façade of the house and is accented with detailed millwork, such as a pediment or curved hood supported by small columns or pilasters. The entrance to a Georgian home usually includes a rectangular or semi-circular transom window above the front door. Glass transom windows remained rectangular until after the American Revolution when the Federal style became popular. Covered porches are rarely incorporated into the design of the façade because of the decorative pediment or hood above the front door.

The windows of a Georgian house are always evenly spaced and in alignment horizontally and vertically. Each sash of the double-hung windows is typically divided into six, nine or twelve small panes. Exterior shutters were a prominent feature of the Georgian style homes; however, they did not appear on every house.

Regional Georgian Styles

The design elements of all Georgian style homes follow the same aesthetic principles and architectural precedents established during the Renaissance. Georgian architecture, regardless of the geographic location, always consists of variations of the same basic design concepts and fundamental components. Variations of the Georgian style are often a reflection of the cultural heritage of the region and the availability of building materials.

In the northeastern region, the gambrel roof is a common feature of Georgian style homes. Georgian houses in New England are traditionally wood-framed with clapboard exterior siding and a paneled front door flanked by classically ordered pilasters that support a pedimented entablature. A transom window above the entrance door is usually either rectangular or semi-circular in shape. Windows on the lower floor match the size of the upper story openings and are typically comprised of relatively small glass panes. Upper floor windows are situated beneath a classically proportioned cornice directly below the eave. The soffit is usually decorated with modillions.

Further south, in the middle-Atlantic colonies, stone or brick was a more common building material for construction of Georgian style homes. These Georgian homes typically feature heavier moldings and details. Gabled roofs are common and cornices below the roof are often decorated with modillions or dentil work. Windows are double-hung and usually contained six glass panes in both the upper and lower sashes. However, variations of the double-hung windows sometimes featured nine or twelve panes of glass in the lower sash.

In the southern colonies, brick was the most commonly used material to construct Georgian homes. Exterior brick walls were laid in the Flemish bond pattern. The main floor of many colonial Georgian homes was elevated above the ground with exterior stairs to the entrance. Roofs on these Georgian houses were generally hipped. The cornice, placed immediately below the eave of the roof, was always classically proportioned with modillions for detailing. Occasionally, a pedimented entrance at the center of the façade included a rectangular or semi-circular transom window above the front door. Window panes were generally small.

The two-story rectangular shape of the traditional Georgian home offers opportunities for a variety of interior layouts. Wings are easily appended to the sides and rear of the house to provide additional living space. When constructed with a gabled roof, windows in the end walls at the attic level provide light and ventilation for additional bedrooms, a playroom, home office, or studio. The symmetric Georgian façade is elegantly simple. The central entrance is often embellished with stately architectural appointments.

The adaptability and expandability of the Georgian home combine classical exterior design with flexibility of the interior layout. Georgian residential architecture remains one of the most popular and timeless styles for American homes.

West Indies Style

(1750-1860)

The islands of the West Indies, situated between the Caribbean Sea and Atlantic Ocean, were colonized by Spain, France, England, Denmark and Holland beginning in the 15th century. The plantations constructed by the colonists were large homes that were relatively simple in architectural detail and ornamentation. Traders and sailors returned home from the West Indies with new building concepts. They employed their knowledge of island construction to erect homes of similar design.

In the American South, West Indies-style residential architecture predates the monumental plantation structures of the Greek Revival period and contrasts with the even greater grandeur of the Neoclassical style. Similar to other Plantation homes built in the South prior to the Neoclassical period, the West Indies style appeared relatively unpretentious.

Cultural exchange resulting from trading between the port of New Orleans and the West Indies prompted development of West Indies-style homes in Louisiana. For this reason, plantation homes built in the West Indies style have also been described as Louisiana Colonial architecture. The island climate of the West Indies was similar to the warm, humid Southern colonies and this style of building performed exceptionally well. The distinctive roof design provides practical shelter from the hot summer sun and frequent rain in the Southern climate.

While early West Indies-style homes were simple and practical in design, their appearance was often exotic. The oldest documented West Indies style plantation home in the Mississippi River valley is Destrehan, built in phases beginning in 1787. The floor plan of the West Indies home allowed for cross ventilation of each room. Wide, wrap-around galleries, or verandas, often surrounded the home creating outdoor spaces that allowed windows to remain open during inclement weather and provide comfort during rainstorms.

Distinctive architectural features of West Indies style include round columns at the ground floor level supporting a main floor gallery with smaller round columns above to support the overhanging roof. The narrow, elongated scale of the main floor columns make the upper story look taller and more elegant, while the columns below at the ground floor are shorter with less refined detailing.

A massive, high-pitched roof is a fundamental design element of a West Indies plantation home. The roof structure is often so tall that it equals the height of the house below. A large exterior staircase provides access to the main floor gallery and entertaining areas. Deep galleries surrounding the elegant main floor living quarters allow cool breezes to enter the house. These galleries also provide outdoor living areas sheltered from rainstorms. Service areas located below at the ground floor level are always constructed of brick or stone to protect the structure from periodic flooding by nearby waterways.

Windows and doors of West Indies homes are simple and similar to Southern plantations of the Acadian style. Glass window panes were small at the time because large pieces of glass were scarce in the New World. Louvered shutters provide a decorative element and a useful means of allowing light and fresh air into the home, while at the same time keeping rain and birds out of the house. Dormer windows commonly appear on the roof to provide light and ventilation in attic rooms.

Parlange Plantation in New Roads, Louisiana is another fine example of West Indies style. This plantation home is comprised of two stories with ground floor service areas built of masonry below the main floor level. The principal living quarters are located at the second or main floor level with a tall, high-pitched roof creating attic spaces that nearly double the volume of interior living area. The interior of Parlange Plantation features carved wood details around the doors, window frames and on ceiling moldings. These distinctive elements of the West Indies style continue to be an integral part of Southern architectural design.

Destrehan Plantation on the Mississippi River features a massive double-pitched roof that is characteristic of the West Indies style of architecture. A wide veranda, extending around all four sides of the house, is accessible from every room on the main floor. Operable French doors provide light and allow cool breezes from the river to flow through the house. Ancillary spaces on the ground floor were originally subject to flooding when the river overflowed its banks prior to the construction of levees. Two-story wings were added at either end of the house to provide additional living quarters.

Federal Style

(1780-1830)

The Federal style of American architecture was an adaptation of an English style popularized by two Scottish brothers, Robert and James Adam, during the late 1700s and early 1800s. This approach to architectural design was called the Federal style in America because it was popular with the leaders of the new nation after the American Revolution.

American homes constructed in the Federal style were located primarily in and around urban areas of the east. This style was popular for approximately 40 years until the Greek Revival style took root in the United States and became a symbol of the democratic ideals of the young nation. Today, the design elements that characterized Federal and Georgian architecture are intertwined because of the eclectic nature of current trends in residential building.

The "Adam" style of classical European architecture featured graceful proportions and an elegant simplicity reminiscent of the preceding Georgian style; however, it is distinctive. A Federal home is easily recognizable and differentiated from a Georgian structure because Federal architecture tends to have more delicate and refined decorative elements than Georgian detailing. Surface treatments are simpler and less ornate. Federal homes have more subtle formal architectural ornamentation and proportional rhythm in their design. The neoclassical aspects of Palladian architecture also impacted the design of Federal-style homes.

During their time, the architectural designs of Robert and James Adam may have been as influential as the Palladian movement was during the 16th century. Robert Adam traveled from Scotland to Italy to study the Roman ruins and was inspired by the colorful interiors, shapes and proportions of rooms. He created a sophisticated interpretation of the architectural details and ornamentation displayed in classical architecture. By utilizing these design elements in his buildings, Robert Adam gained great popularity both in England and America.

Federal homes often have two full stories plus a shorter attic story that combines with the roof structure to make the house seem very tall.

The width of the façade typically approximates its height, giving the front elevation a square or slightly rectangular proportion. Brick is the most common exterior building material for Federal-style homes. In the north, wood siding is frequently used instead of brick. Stone quoins are often provided to highlight the corners of the house.

Slender decorative chimneys are prominently displayed on low-pitched gabled roofs or the hipped roof of a Federal-style home. A decorative balustrade often accentuates the ridge of a hipped roof or surrounds the entire roof above the eave. The Federal-style roof is often so low-pitched that it is hardly visible behind a balustrade placed above the eave. Simple brick belt courses placed on the exterior of some Federal style homes identify the floor levels within the house.

The front entrance to a Federal-style home is often covered by a small portico that is supported by columns or pilasters of a classical order. The front door is usually decorated with wood panels. Semi-circular and elliptical fan light transoms first appeared on Federal-style homes to adorn the main entrance. Glass side lights are also common features for the Federal-style front entry.

Double-hung sash windows extending to the floor and rising to standard window height are a distinctive feature of Federal-style architecture. This design configuration causes the proportions of a Federal-style window to seem taller and elegantly slender. Windows are typically divided into six panes per sash and separated by thin muntins. The upper sash of the Federal-style window is generally rectangular; however, brick work is sometimes arched at the top of Southern Federal windows. Feature windows at the center of the façade on the upper floor are ofter arched top or Palladian style openings. Exterior blinds or shutters are a common feature on Federal-style windows.

The classical nature of Federal design elements give the style a timeless quality that ensures its continuing popularity as an American residential style.

Greek Revival

(1825-1860)

The Greek Revival style of architecture became a symbol of American democratic ideals at the beginning of the 19th century. The classical proportions and traditional architectural design elements of the Greek Revival style included classically ordered columns and elegant detailing that were reminiscent of well-formed ancient architecture. Greek architecture also symbolized the philosophy of democratic government.

Greek Revival architecture is said to have been the first style to achieve national prominence in America. Design elements were derived from British examples of Greek Revival architecture. Between 1820 and 1850 the Greek Revival style of architecture flourished across the country, during a time of rapid expansion. Greek Revival was the design of choice for government buildings in Philadelphia and Washington, state capitols, majestic southern plantation homes and residences throughout the northeast and mid-west.

Greek Revival architecture is a Neoclassical style based upon the ancient Greek rules of scale and proportion for buildings. While the term Neoclassical refers to new interpretations of classical ancient Roman and Greek architecture, the Greek Revival in America focused specifically on the Greek orders: Doric, Ionic and Corinthian rules of proportion and ornamentation. Greek Revival residences and public buildings are distinguished by symmetrical façades constructed of stucco, smooth masonry or stone.

Special features of a Greek Revival façade often include a monumental portico having a row of two-story columns supporting a low-pitched triangular pediment similar in design to a Greek temple. Unlike Roman architecture, arches are seldom incorporated into a Greek Revival exterior design. Other features characterizing this style are decorative friezes and cornices, engaged pilasters and a window inset in the pediment (front gable). Below the pediment, a wide entablature extending across the column capitols gracefully supports the roof structure. The front door of the Greek Revival home is often flanked by side lights and pilasters adorned above with a rectangular transom or decorative pediment.

As the Greek Revival style spread across America, the design elements were also adapted to structures in small towns and rural areas. The influence of this style transcended economic barriers through simplification of design and changes in materials to create rural farmhouses and modest urban residences. These homes and buildings featured simplified design details often fabricated in wood rather than stone or masonry. A wide cornice banding the structure below the eave of the roof was substituted for the Greek entablature. Clapboard (wood) siding was often applied for exterior wall surfaces and engaged pilasters were substituted at the corners for columns on the façade. End gables were designed to emulate Greek pediments and shutters were attached to embellish window openings.

The amazing adaptability of this style of ancient Greek architecture, rediscovered during the Renaissance, had been transformed by European architects into stately manor houses and public buildings. Centuries later, English architects brought the Greek Revival style to America where it flourished as the first national style of the young republic. The stately elegance of Greek Revival architecture that first appeared in America nearly 200 years ago has become a symbol of the government. The Greek Revival style was chosen for the United States Supreme Court building designed by architect Cass Gilbert in the 1930s as a reflection of the ideals of Greek democracy and the fundamental principals upon which this nation was founded. Examples of Greek Revival architecture can be found in almost every major American city, whether in the form of public buildings or private residences.

Elements of the Greek Revival continue to influence residential architecture and interior design in remarkable ways ranging from undetectable subtleties to the strict symmetry of a carefully articulated and well-proportioned façade. The influence of the ancient Greeks is so pervasive that it is practically impossible to find a well-appointed room devoid of any classical design element or pattern. Classic design elements can be found today in everything from ceiling moldings to stone floor patterns and furnishings to fabrics.

Southern Plantations

(mid-1700s-1860)

The subtropical climate of the lower Mississippi region spurred settlers to develop a new form of eclectic architecture. The river provided access for early development and farming in Louisiana and Mississippi, while annual flooding of lands adjacent to the river fertilized the soil for crops. Abundant trees and other indigenous resources provided building materials. The character of the land and available building materials strongly influenced the methods of construction. The Carolina "Low Country" underwent a similar development pattern.

Plantation home design incorporated the unique ecology of the South and the needs for both housing and management of substantial farming operations. Plantation homes were usually larger than houses built in towns and cities due to their remote locations. They required self-dependence because rural farms lacked the goods and services available in urban areas. Early plantation homes were basic in design with simple details. However, later examples featured elaborate ornamental detailing and refined architectural designs.

European social customs inherited by many plantation owners produced formal homes of a classic design. The Southern plantation home often included a central hallway flanked by living quarters on the main floor. Seasonal flooding from nearby rivers required that the main floor living spaces be raised above a ground floor comprised of cooking and service areas. Wrap-around porches, sometimes surrounding the entire residence of the plantation homes in the Deep South, were designed for outdoor living and built deep enough to provide protection from the hot summer sun and frequent rain.

Southern plantation homes were designed in several different architectural styles. The earlier colonial styles reflected simple French and English architectural design characteristics. As the South prospered from a rich agrarian economy, the plantation homes evolved from the modest designs of the early settlers into stately mansions. Two of the finest examples of Georgian style plantation homes are Drayton Hall in South Carolina and Carter's Grove in Virginia, both constructed in the mid-1700s.

In the late 1700s Neoclassical architecture, based upon ancient Roman and Greek rules of design, became fashionable in America. This has been attributed in part to an appreciation for the Greek democracy that was a popular model for the American form of government. Greek Revival detailing, massive porticos, tall classic columns and wide wrap-around verandas were gracefully incorporated into the design of many prominent Southern plantation homes. Variations on the Southern plantation-style home are still constructed today.

The design of the original plantation homes often included a ground floor with low ceilings built of materials that could withstand repeated flooding and could quickly be restored to habitable condition. Brick or flagstone floors and masonry walls served this purpose in plantation homes near rivers. The main floor living areas, like the *piano nobile* of the Venetian villas, were elevated one story above the ground. Living rooms and family quarters featured high ceilings, elaborate design details and the finest interior finishes and furnishings. In some cases, bedrooms were also provided at the third floor or attic level.

Many plantation homes featured grand staircases either on the façade to create an impressive entrance to the main floor, or within the foyer as a gracefully curving stairway to the upper floor. The image of the plantation home is synonymous with the concept of elegant living and the shape or massing of the structure is easily adaptable to a virtually infinite variety of interior floor plans.

The versatility of the Southern plantation style is enhanced by the ability to add symmetrical wings to each side of the main house. This feature provides the opportunity to incorporate garages, ground floor master suites, utility areas, storage and workshops without disturbing the layout of formal areas on the ground floor.

When designing a new two-story Southern plantation home, the scale and proportion of the façade are vitally important. While the original plantation homes were often inverted in plan with entertaining areas at the second floor level, recent examples of this style place the living areas on the ground floor with bedrooms upstairs. This reversal of the floor plan inverts the proportions of the front elevation. If the home features columns and a second floor balcony on the façade, the lower ceiling height is further diminished by the disproportionate height of the balcony railing between columns and the large cornice, called an entablature, spanning horizontally across the tops of the columns. Conversely, ceiling height between columns at the ground floor level is exaggerated by the taller living areas on the first floor.

The adaptability of the Southern plantation style to floor plans that address contemporary lifestyles contributes to its continuing popularity. However, it is always important to incorporate the ancient rules of scale and proportion that created the classical architecture from which the magnificent Southern plantations were derived.

Italian Architecture

(1830-1935)

The Italian style of architecture is a remarkable reflection of the wealth, talent, diverse history and culture of Italy. From its origin in ancient Rome, Italian architecture has evolved through the enlightenment of the Renaissance, the opulent Baroque period and the simplicity of contemporary interpretations of classical styles. Throughout this evolution, Italian architecture has retained a distinct appearance that is easily identified when compared to other styles.

Design elements that characterize distinctly Italian architectural features include the campanile, belvedere and heavily bracketed cornices. Italian residential architecture includes vibrant colors and rich patterns, integrated into well-proportioned, stately structures. Italian architecture typically includes the use of a heavy cornice with brackets or dentils, a low pitched or flat roof, restrained and dignified ornamentation and simple building materials such as stone masonry or scored stucco.

Italian architecture became a prevalent style in America shortly before the Civil War. Italian architecture was extremely popular in areas of the United States that experienced significant growth during the mid-to-late 1800s. Homes constructed in this style proliferated in the midwest, parts of the northeast and in some areas of California. The Italian architectural style eventually became more popular in America than the fashionable Greek Revival and Gothic Revival styles.

The Italian style of architecture is usually classified into three categories: Italianate, Italian Villa and Italian Renaissance Revival. Italianate-style residences were particularly popular in urbanized areas of the northeast, while the Italian Villa style represented country homes. The Italian Renaissance Revival style frequently appeared in the design of American public buildings. Although these classifications differ in many ways, it is easy to identify each as an Italian-style building.

Italian Renaissance Revival

(1880s-1920s)

The Italian Renaissance Revival style of architecture features design characteristics influenced by the palaces and public buildings built during the Renaissance period in Tuscany and northern Italy. Architecture of the Italian Renaissance was designed to discourage intrusion and symbolize status, making the scale of the structures impressive. The Italian Revival style was popular from the 1880s through the 1920s and features simple, flat façades, formal and restrained ornamentation and horizontal, rectangular forms. The Italian Renaissance Revival style was often used for men's clubs from 1880 through the 1920s. The Italian Renaissance Revival style is often utilized for the design of row houses and townhouses in large, densely populated cities.

Homes built in this style are highly symmetrical, very formal and typically feature a heavy cornice decorated with dentils or modillions that wraps around the house. However, only the façade of townhouses or row houses is usually decorated with a heavy cornice. The piano nobile, or main floor, is generally situated at the second floor level. A monumental exterior staircase often ascends to a grand porch providing access to the main entrance.

Few Italian Renaissance Revival-style residences include columns in the exterior design. These homes have more restrained and classical ornamentation and decoration than houses built in the Italian Villa style. Exterior design details include heavy rustication (stone blocks or scored stucco) on the ground floor, quoins (stacked corner blocks) and arched, hooded windows. The Italian Renaissance style residence was always constructed of stone or brick covered with stucco.

The Italian Renaissance roof structure is typically hipped, low-pitched and understated by comparison to the rest of the exterior design. The roof is usually covered with terra-cotta tile and overhangs the exterior walls creating broad eaves. A large and prominent entablature appears below the eave of Italian Renaissance buildings. The entablature is classically proportioned to the height of the building.

The main floor windows of an Italian Renaissance residence are taller and more decoratively ornate than windows on other levels. Exterior windows and doors on an Italian Renaissance residence are usually positioned in a symmetrical arrangement on the principal façade. The front door of an Italian Renaissance home is often decorated with an intricately designed frame and accented with ornamentation that may include a pediment supported by small columns or pilasters.

The lower floor level of the Italian Renaissance residence is often partially submerged below grade. The ground floor walls are commonly finished in a heavily rusticated block design. Quoin blocks are frequently employed as a decorative element on the façade. String or belt courses on the exterior walls circumscribe the structure to distinguish the different floor levels.

The formal elegance of the Italian Renaissance Revival style, with its classical ornamentation and restrained decoration, derives its architectural design characteristics from the finest palaces and public buildings built in central and northern Italy during the 16th century. In America, this style became more popular for townhouses and public facilities than single family residences. The typical stone construction and partially submerged lower floor of the Italian Renaissance Revival style made it more conducive to northern construction than for structures in the South.

Italian Villa Style

(1840s-1880s)

Originally, the Italian Villa was an irregular, asymmetrical shaped residence with a tower or campanile on the principle façade that was a defining characteristic of this style. The tower was often placed off-center so as to enhance the asymmetric design of the façade and to provide a charming architectural element. The lack of demand for symmetry in Italian Villa design allowed the architect to concentrate on developing a functional plan by focusing particular attention on the manner in which interior spaces flowed from one room to another. The Italian Villa style is easily distinguished by the use of elaborately ornate brackets on the soffit below the eaves of the roof and the campanile towering above an asymmetrical façade.

Italian Villa-style homes built in America during the mid-1800s were designed to emulate manor houses of the Italian countryside. Villas tended to be larger than cottages and more organized than farm houses. They were considered to be the perfect size for a family residence. Although Italian Villa-style homes were generally rambling and irregular in plan, they were cohesive in design with a carefully developed layout that was efficient and comfortable for the residents. Influential pattern books encouraged builders to construct Italianate and Italian Villa-style homes in America.

Italian Villa-style homes frequently include a square tower, or campanile, on the main façade of the structure. This element makes the Italian Villa style easily distinguishable from other types of Italian architecture. The main house is typically comprised of two stories above the ground with a tower rising 1 to 1-1/2 additional floors, accentuating verticality. The Italian Villa roof is a low-pitched hipped structure having large, overhanging eaves covered with terra-cotta tiles.

As with other Italian styles, Italian Villas have a heavy band called the entablature that runs horizontally around the building below the roof overhang. Massive, ornate brackets that support the projecting eaves of the roof occur either in pairs or separately on the soffit below the roof overhang.

The composition of Italian Villa-style homes can be either symmetrical or asymmetrical in an L- or T-shaped plan. Italian Villa-style homes frequently feature a pediment incorporated into the design of the façade, either atop the tower element or above the main house to add prominence. A long, one-story porch typically runs across the principal façade or a veranda wraps around a portion of the Italian Villa-style residence.

Windows of Italian Villa-style homes are often tall and arched at the top but they can also be rectangular in shape. Decorative pediments, cornices, crowns or hoods are set above the windows to embellish the design. Italian Villa-style homes commonly feature arched windows set in pairs or sets of three, especially on the tower. However, it is just as common to see the windows placed individually. Bay windows are also typical adornments.

The front entrance to an Italian Villa-style home can have either a single or double door that is often highly ornate and decorative. The front door is often adorned with side and transom windows. These windows are typically rectangular in shape, rather than the fan shape frequently seen in the Federal style.

Italian Villa-style homes were constructed primarily in urbanized areas of the United States during the mid-to-late 1800s. The dramatic composition of this architectural style, with its imposing towers, ornately bracketed eaves and terra-cotta tile roofs offers an intriguing complement to the tailored and predictable Colonial, Georgian and Federal styles. The design elements of the Italian Villa style are difficult to apply to modest homes and houses constructed on small lots.

Italianate Architecture

(1840s-1880s)

Italianate architecture first appeared in America in the 1840s contemporaneously with the Picturesque movement in England that departed from the formality of classical architecture. The Italianate home remained the leading style for American residences until the 1880s. Drawing inspiration from the Tuscan late-Medieval farmhouses, the Italianate style was especially popular in cities and towns that were experiencing tremendous growth during this period. Construction of these homes was particularly common in the Midwest, San Francisco and in northeastern cities on the seacoast. The Italianate style cornice embellished the façade of townhouses in urban areas.

In the suburbs and rural settings, Italianate style homes were rarely custom designed because builders could easily find Italian-inspired plans in popular pattern books or they would simply add Italianate details to an exterior façade. These homes were similar to the houses built in the Italian Villa style; however, they did not include a tower or campanile and often featured less complex detailing. Homes built in the Italianate style featured a traditional low-pitched hipped roof that was often topped by a cupola or lantern. Other typical design elements include deep cornices with elaborately detailed brackets and tall windows that were frequently curved or arched at the top.

Italianate-style homes were generally constructed of the most abundant building material in the area. Italianate homes were typically wood-framed structures with a stucco finish and stone or wood detailing. Stone masonry was also used as an exterior building material to construct Italianate-style homes. The exterior surface material on the principal façade traditionally has a smooth finish.

Italianate homes frequently have small, one-story entry porches. The front porch is typically supported by square columns or pilasters that usually appear individually or in pairs. A heavy entablature is a typical design element of an Italianate building. The cornice and frieze are ornately decorated with elaborate brackets that support the broadly overhanging eaves. Brackets enhancing the entablature of an Italianate residence are always evenly spaced and can be placed individually or in pairs.

Italianate homes are often box-shaped, having square plans typically consisting of two or three stories above the ground. Attic level spaces in Italianate homes have small windows that appear from the exterior to be set into the wide cornice. The position of these windows below the roof provides an opportunity for additional detailing of the entablature and adds extra ceiling height in rooms at the third floor level. These windows also provide ventilation for the house during the summer months.

Italianate style residences characteristically include arched windows with ornate hoods or crowns. However, rectangular-shaped windows are also appropriate to this style. Windows are commonly arranged in pairs or sets of three. Italianate-style windows are often double hung and comprised of two large panes of glass.

Italianate style doors, like the windows, are elaborately decorated and appear in both arched top or rectangular shapes. Double doors are a popular feature for the main entrance to an Italianate home. Entrance doors are usually intricately adorned with paneling in sophisticated designs. Doors and windows of an Italianate residence are placed in a symmetrical arrangement on the principal façade.

The Italianate style dominated American residential design in the Northeast, Midwest and parts of California for nearly half a century. Builders easily adapted the style to a variety of layouts, and the Italianate design features could be copied from plan books and integrated into residential developments in rapidly growing urban areas. By the early 20th century, Victorian architectural styles became popular and interest in Italianate designs waned.

The Victorian Period

(1837-1901)

The Victorian period extended over the sixty-four years of Queen Victoria's reign and included a broad spectrum of architectural styles. A popular misconception about Victorian architecture is that it is one particular type of building. In fact, it is a period of history encompassing many architectural styles. Early Victorian styles of this era include the Gothic Revival and Italianate. In the second half of the century, Second Empire, Romanesque Revival, Eastlake Victorian and Queen Anne were popular. In the Northeast, the Shingle style emerged during the latter half of the Victorian period as a reaction to the excessive ornamentation of the Queen Anne and Eastlake styles. It was the beginning of a new era in architectural design during which many different residential styles emerged.

During the early Victorian period, so called "Gothick" designs based on medieval architecture became the preferred style for new residences in England. This movement symbolized a rejection of the formality of classic Renaissance architecture and quickly spread to America. The Gothic Revival style of architecture became fashionable in America for approximately forty years, beginning about 1840. Special features of this style were adapted from medieval Gothic cathedrals. Most of the early Gothic Revival structures were stone buildings, churches or boldly detailed estates with pointed arches, carved stonework, crenelation and parapets. The impressive height of these homes was accentuated vertically by gabled roofs, cast iron crestings, groups of chimneys and pinnacles.

As the Gothic Revival style grew in popularity, wooden ornamentation known as "gingerbread" replaced the expensive masonry details. Modest homes were designed, often asymmetrically, with steep gables and pointed windows to emulate the dramatic verticality of the Gothic Revival. Loggias, towers and porches were abundant. These wood-framed homes became known as stick style or "Carpenter Gothic," and were often clad with vertical board and batten siding to emphasize their height. At its height, Victorian Gothic encompassed the stick style. "Stick" design highlighted post-and-beam construction, including ornamental trusses, exposed rafter ends or bracing and patterned wall surfaces. Towers, wings and gables were also prevalent. The stick style was a precursor to the later Queen Anne style.

The Italianate style gained widespread popularity after the Civil War, drawing design precedents from the historic architecture of Tuscany and the Lombard region of northern Italy. One of the most common features of Italianate architecture is the wide roof overhang with bracketed eaves. Other characteristics of this style include a symmetrical façade, semi-circular arched-top windows, multi-story rectangular shape, paired doors and a low-pitched roof often featuring a rectangular or square cupola.

The Second Empire style came into vogue between the mid-nineteenth century and 1885, emulating the ornate French architecture associated with the reign of Napoleon III. The Parisian influence of Second Empire features a mansard roof forming the outer wall of the upper story attic area, almost equal in size to the floor below. Dormer windows in the nearly vertical mansard roof, forming the perimeter walls at the attic level, provide light and ventilation for the interior living areas. A low-pitched or flat roof above these attic rooms covers the structure, spanning between mansard roof elements. Other features of Second Empire include paired columns, bulls-eye windows, iron cresting at the ridges of the roof, brackets below the eaves, bay windows and balconies.

During the same period that Second Empire residential architecture was a notable American style, Eastlake Victorian gained popularity. Named for English furniture designer Charles Eastlake, the spindled columns, knobs, buttons and decorative woodwork on gables, brackets, fascia moldings, eaves and friezes are attributed to Eastlake designs. Its ornamental details also appear on other Victorian residential styles, including Queen Anne and embellishments to the Stick style of timber and shingle exterior designs in wood. The advent of the Industrial Age made the replication of these details affordable to the masses and resulted in a proliferation of ornamental detailing never seen before in residential architecture.

The Romanesque Revival style of Victorian architecture was characterized by the heavy appearance of wide round arches, short stocky columns and rough-faced exterior stone walls. Also referred to as the Richardsonian style, this architectural form was originated by Boston architect Henry Hobson Richardson. Towers, eyebrow dormer windows and carved floral details are also prominent design elements of this style. Other distinguishing features are vaults, massive walls and windows in a variety of shapes and sizes. Deep window reveals, contrasting exterior textures and material colors and terra-cotta tile roofs usually appeared on these homes. Romanesque Revival homes were expensive to construct, restricting the style to wealthy individuals and limiting its popularity to a short period from 1870 to 1900.

Queen Anne houses feature the most elaborate detailing of the Victorian residential styles. Products of the industrial revolution included mass-manufactured architectural woodwork and trim stimulating the creative ingenuity and self-expression of architects, builders and craftsmen. Queen Anne became fashionable as Eastlake Victorian was fading in the 1880s. Queen Anne style reigned as the prominent building style for the next twenty to thirty years. Prominent features of Queen Anne include elaborate ornamental "gingerbread" woodwork that was characteristic of the Gothic Revival style, steep irregular-shaped roofs with gable ends, towers, turrets, bay windows, wrap-around porches and balconies. The irregular symmetrical shape of Queen Anne reflects a floor plan that has been developed from the inside and subsequently fitted with an exterior design. Row houses on the east and west coasts often exhibit Queen Anne styling, ranging from New York brownstones to the intricate and colorful woodwork of the attached homes on the hillsides of San Francisco. Many distinctive examples of the Queen Anne style stand prominently today in residential neighborhoods throughout the country.

The Victorian era was one of the most diverse and creative periods in American architectural history. The combined influences of the Industrial Revolution, economic prosperity and unprecedented capital formation fostered prolific architectural expression, innovation and ostentation. The result is a remarkable collection of residential architecture that continues to delight residents, tourists and historians.

French Architecture

(1918-1960)

Following World War I, many veterans who served in France developed an affinity for rural French homes. This style took root in the U.S. as Americans emulated the French architecture of Normandy and Brittany when planning their own homes. Books about French homes published during this period also stimulated the construction of American homes in this style. French-style homes include a wide array of shapes and construction materials with differing styles of ornamental embellishment and design details. Prominent characteristics of French residential architecture include steeply pitched hipped roofs with dormer windows accenting the design.

Some French homes feature design elements similar to the Medieval architecture of England. The French houses of Normandy with half-timbering resemble the English Tudor style, particularly the use of exterior materials and steep roof design. In contrast, homes of the Second Empire style are boxy and feature the distinctive mansard roof. French Provincial architecture is generally asymmetrical in design and sometimes features a cylindrical tower on the façade. French Provincial homes are often informal in style. Important elements of the Beaux Arts style of French architecture include elegant Renaissance details and a generally symmetric façade design.

Common features of French-style homes in America are steep roofs, flared eaves and segmented arched doorways. Because of the returning veterans' desire for rural French style, the majority of French-style residences in America are an eclectic mixture of design elements from the homes of Brittany and Normandy.

Second Empire

(1855-1880)

The Second Empire style of Parisian French architecture flourished during the reign of Napoleon III around 1850. The Second Empire style was also popular in America for about 30 years, beginning at the same time.

The most dramatic characteristic of the Second Empire style is the steeply pitched roof designed by François Mansart that appears to be almost vertical and forms the outside wall of the upper level. Patterned slate in a variety of colors often decorated the mansard roof surface. Named for its designer, the mansard roof creates an upper floor area almost the size of the lower floors. The top surface of the mansard roof is practically flat where it covers the upper story. The exceptionally large volume of attic space enveloped by the mansard roof provides additional living space in homes constructed on small lots in urban areas.

Exterior design elements of the Second Empire style include decorative brackets below the eaves, French double doors and narrow arched-top windows similar in shape to Italianate style of an earlier period. The Second Empire style often features a rooftop cupola and unique dormer windows with minimal projection from the roof. Wrought iron cresting installed above the upper cornice of the mansard roof was a design feature used to provide ornamentation. Classical pediments often adorned the dormer windows and appeared at the roof line above projecting bays. One-story porches, balconies and bay windows were also common features of the Second Empire style.

The design for government buildings constructed in the United States during the prosperous first term of President Ulysses Grant often favored the Second Empire style. However, the panic of 1873 and subsequent economic depression until 1877 diminished interest in the opulent Second Empire style.

French Normandy

(1920-1940)

The American adaptation of the French architecture of Normandy emulates the rural farm houses of that region with grain silos attached to the main house. This architectural element is reflected by a cylindrical tower with a cone-shaped roof attached to the façade of the American version, forming the front entrance to the home.

During the latter 19th century, wealthy Americans who traveled in France returned home with a desire to create grand manor houses fashioned after the opulent 16th century chateaux of Normandy and Loire Valley. Belcourt Castle in Rhode Island, built in the French Normandy style, was designed by Richard Morris Hunt, an American architect who received his training in France. The exterior design of Belcourt features half-timbering, an architectural design element that is characteristic of the Normandy style.

After World War I, returning veterans who served in France began constructing smaller versions of the farm houses and manor houses they had seen in Normandy. These eclectic French Normandy homes were affordable for middle class homeowners and the rambling style adapted easily to a wide variety of floor plans. During the 1920s, the French Normandy residential style became popular in the South. In fact, an entire community was built in Asheville, North Carolina exclusively featuring French Normandy-style homes. French Normandy residential architecture simultaneously appeared on the West Coast. These homes often combined the brick and half-timbering of French farm houses with Spanish tile roofs and heavy wood carved details. Vaulted ceilings and iron railings were introduced to the design by California builders.

French Normandy homes were usually constructed of brick, stone or stucco. The exterior walls were often fabricated to appear as if they were built using techniques known as bousillage and briquette-entre-poteaux, where exposed framing members are set in a geometric pattern of square and diagonal timbers, between which the triangular open spaces are filled with brick or stucco. This construction technique resembles the Tudor style of architecture popular in England.

Like French Provincial architecture, the adaptability of the French Normandy style to arrangements in plan and scale makes it an enduring part of American residential architecture.

French Provincial

(1918-1960s)

French Provincial homes evolved during the mid-1600s with the construction of rural manor houses. French Provincial architecture in America is modeled after these manor houses. Similar to those in France, these homes were large and comfortable. It gained popularity in America during the post-war building boom of the 1920s and was again revived in the 1960s.

Rural home design of the French provinces is characteristically simple and understated. The mass of the French Provincial home is dominated by a steeply pitched, hipped roof. In plan, these homes are generally arranged in the form of a one or two story rectangle, or an L-shaped layout with a cylindrical tower serving as the main entrance. Occasionally, the floor plan may consist of a pair of rectangles, differing in size and coupled together, one beside the other.

French Provincial design elements include tall, narrow, rectangular chimneys. Windows are generally simple, accented by an arched top, shutters, or decorative masonry detailing. Slate roofs and copper gutters are key elements of the exterior construction.

A distinctive design element of this style is a second story dormer window that breaks through the eave of the roof, with the face of the dormer becoming a vertical extension of the façade wall below. These windows are usually arched at the top and provide light and ventilation in the attic rooms. The formal French Provincial home is often rectangular in plan with symmetrically balanced windows flanking a central entry portal. Brick or stucco are the most common exterior finish materials. Symmetrically placed chimneys, balconies and galleries with balustrades represent other prominent features of this style.

A well-known example of this style is the Plaza Hotel at Central Park in New York. Its steep-pitched roof articulated with dormer windows and copper details is a dramatic example of the French Provincial influence in America. On a lesser scale, French Provincial homes have remained popular in suburban developments throughout the United States since the 1920s. American architecture classified as French Country is usually an eclectic combination of the rural design elements borrowed from Normandy and the French countryside.

The French Provincial style is adaptable to a variety of layouts in plan. The classic design of French Provincial homes continues to provide an elegant European influence on American residential architecture. This traditional architectural style periodically regains popularity. The scale and proportions of French Provincial homes are well-suited for both estate properties and upscale residential development.

Beaux Arts Style

(1880-1930)

The Beaux Arts style of architecture originated at the École des Beaux Arts (School of Fine Arts) in Paris as a French interpretation of the Neoclassical architectural style. Architects of the Beaux Arts style were expected to be versed in the application of historical design elements and detailing in a variety of architectural styles. Beaux Arts is an eclectic combination of Renaissance designs with ancient Roman and Greek detailing. The Beaux Arts movement gained popularity in France and the United States from 1885-1920s, following the Second Empire style that flourished during the reign of Napoleon III.

Schools of architecture were late in coming to the United States. American universities did not offer architectural education until after the Civil War, beginning with MIT in 1865. Consequently, the educational opportunities provided by École des Beaux Arts attracted American students pursuing architectural careers. Many prominent American architects were trained in Europe. Among them were Richard Morris Hunt and Charles F. McKim, a principal of McKim, Mead and White, the New York firm responsible for the design of many imposing Beaux Arts style residences and numerous public buildings including Grand Central Station and public libraries in Boston and New York. The Lincoln Memorial Opera House and National Gallery in Washington, D.C., Union Station in Chicago and the War Memorial in San Francisco are splendid examples of Beaux Arts architecture in America.

Major residences and public buildings of the Beaux Arts style are characteristically ornamental masonry structures replete with lavish sculptural decoration linked together with other architectural elements and reminiscent of Baroque and Rococo designs. These large sculptural design elements were supported by traditional architectural components including deep cornices, pediments and parapets.

Symmetry is a fundamental characteristic of the Beaux Arts style. Notable decorative design features include grand staircases and entrances, stone columns, pilasters, balustrades, swags, garlands, cartouches, ornamental sculpture and bas-relief on wall panels. While the exterior designs were formal and structured, the internal layouts and circulation patterns were functionally sophisticated and easily discernable.

Prominence of the Beaux Arts architectural style waned at the beginning of World War I as interest in Modernism and the International style began in Europe and began to impact the design of homes and office building in America.

Neoclassical Architecture

(1780-1850s)

Neoclassical architecture is based upon ancient Greek and Roman design principles, rules of scale and proportion and classical orders. This movement began with the works of Andrea Palladio in the 16th century during the Italian Renaissance period. Neoclassical architecture became fashionable in England and France during the 18th century. Neoclassicism was advanced by the French Academy in Rome and is reflected in the design of the Petit Trianon, the Pantheon and the Arc de Triomphe in Paris. At this time, England adopted the architecture of Palladio, inspiring a movement against the excessively ornate Rococo style. Chiswick House in London is a famous example of the Palladian style of Neoclassical architecture.

Neoclassical architecture, like Greek Revival, gained popularity as a symbol of American independence after the War of 1812, acknowledging an appreciation for the ancient Greek system of democratic government. Pattern books from England offered classical ornamental detailing that could be used to embellish architectural design elements on new residences including columns, pilasters, cornices, pediments, moldings and exterior fenestration, that is, doors and windows.

Prominent characteristics of Neoclassical architecture are dramatic façades featuring two-story columns forming a portico, low-pitched triangular pediments, symmetrically balanced front elevations, Greek or Roman ornamental design elements and use of the classical orders: Doric, Ionic and Corinthian. Neoclassical residences and buildings are often of a grand scale and occasionally feature domed roofs.

The Neoclassical Revival in America influenced a number of architectural styles. Among these styles were the stately antebellum Southern plantation homes, symmetrically balanced and classically detailed Federal-style residences, Greek Revival-style homes and the elegantly appointed Beaux Arts buildings constructed toward the end of the 19th century.

After the American Revolution, interest in the Georgian style waned, prompting the pervasive influence of Neoclassical architecture on American residential design for more than a hundred years. The Federal style of traditional classicism was prevalent in the Northeast while the Mid-Atlantic works of Thomas Jefferson were based primarily on Roman architecture. In Washington, D.C., architect Benjamin Latrobe used stone building techniques to create monumental Neoclassical structures with massive classical vaults and domes. By 1820, interest in the Greek Revival style of Neoclassical architecture was sweeping the country. It became the first nationally recognized architectural style, influencing the design of every building type from farmhouses to statehouses and flourishing until the 1850s. The Beaux Arts style, a French interpretation of classical design, appeared from 1885-1920, near the end of the Neoclassical period of American architecture.

Neoclassical design elements are applicable to both large and small residences and buildings, demonstrating the remarkable versatility and adaptability of these ancient precepts for architectural design. The stately proportions and elegant simplicity of Neoclassical architecture provide seemingly endless residential design opportunities. Neoclassical architectural appointments can be replicated and fabricated from an assortment of building materials ranging from natural stone to cast concrete, plaster, brick, wood and dense molded polyfoam synthetics.

Neoclassical structures are comprised of simple forms that allow easy application of the selected design features to create the desired architectural composition. Neoclassical architecture embraces the generous use of broad, flat exterior wall surfaces spanning between openings. The application of decorative relief work is usually concentrated at the edges of the roof, corners of the structure and on cornices or mouldings surrounding openings. Simple rural homes often feature Neoclassical detailing on the gable ends of the roof with engaged pilasters at the corners of the building.

Today, many Neoclassical residential designs constructed after World War II are classified as "traditional architecture." These homes usually feature classical design elements applied to the front elevation creating a reference to Neoclassical design through the use of symmetrically balanced windows on a two-story façade, a central portico with tall columns, an elaborate front door surround and eave mouldings. Traditional homes displaying Neoclassical design elements are often eclectic in composition.

The ancient Romans and Greeks created a timeless architecture that spread to every continent over a period of two thousand years. It is remarkable that the elements of classical architecture possess such widespread appeal and functionality. Classical principles of architectural design re-emerged during the Renaissance and were reinterpreted in the 18th century. Neoclassical architecture was the chosen style for our nation's capital city and appeared again in the form of Post-Modernism toward the end of the 20th century. Few nations are devoid of classical buildings. New architectural expressions of classical designs foster the creation of elegant homes, stately manor houses, villas, embassies and palaces around the world.

Mediterranean Style

(1900-1930)

The Mediterranean style is an American adaptation and revival of European architecture from the seacoasts of Italy, France and Spain. The design of seaside mansions and resorts overlooking the Mediterranean featured tile roofs, stucco walls with arched entry porticos and large covered porches. Casement windows, stone floors and rustic iron hardware are among the special features that characterize traditional Mediterranean architecture.

As the American economy flourished during the 1920s, opportunities were created for commercial and residential development by the construction of railroad lines to Florida and the Gulf Coast. Major hotels were erected near these railroad lines along the Atlantic coast and Gulf of Mexico. Hotel buildings were constructed, many of them in the Mediterranean style, to lure visitors from the north. As a result, new towns boomed in this American version of the chic European Riviera.

A similar revival of the Mediterranean style, also emulating the European Riviera, appeared along the Pacific coast in California. Railroads in California used the Mediterranean style for the design of train depots. Spanish influences from Central and South America were integrated to create eclectic regional styles of Mediterranean architecture both in Florida and California.

Although the Mediterranean style first appeared in the design of hotels and commercial buildings, it also became a popular residential style for seaside mansions. The homes and hotels of the Mediterranean seacoast are primarily multi-story, rectangular in plan and generally symmetrically balanced in exterior design. While post-war residences and resorts in America incorporate similar design features including stucco walls, terra-cotta roofs, balconies and elaborate door surrounds, the massing of these new homes is often significantly modified to meet market demands. New golfing communities abound with Mediterranean residential design elements adorning angular geometric configurations oriented toward available views of the links or waterfront. The symmetry and rectangular geometry that characterized the original multi-story Mediterranean resort homes are often modified to create smaller homes.

Special features of Mediterranean-style homes include stucco exterior walls, low-pitched terra-cotta barrel tile roofs, arch-topped windows and portals and detailed masonry relief work surrounding heavily carved wooden doors. Other features prominently integrated into the Mediterranean style in Florida were derived from the Spanish colonial heritage including wrought iron balconies and stucco walls topped with terracotta tile. Private walled gardens were also a popular feature.

The Mediterranean style is interpreted differently in each region of America, just as stylistic variations originally developed in the countries forming the southern European seacoast. In America, Mediterranean style homes are generally Italian Renaissance Revival residences located along the seacoast. Practical features of the Mediterranean style fare well in the sunny coastal areas of Florida and California with broad eave overhangs to provide shade for windows and terra-cotta roofing that withstands the deleterious effects of intense sunlight. Mediterranean balconies, porches and loggia are ideal for outdoor living in the mild east and western seacoast climates. Early Mediterranean-style mansions in Florida and California are among the most fascinating and magnificent examples of the American interpretation of this intriguing European architectural style.

Prominent architects designing outstanding Mediterranean-style homes and buildings in Florida during the 1920s were Addison Mizner, August Geiger and the firm of Carrere and Hastings. In California, Summer Spalding and Paul Williams created Mediterranean residences that incorporated Spanish and classic historical architectural details. Unfortunately, in 1929 the onslaught of the Great Depression ended this remarkable period of American architecture. Other styles became popular as the nation recovered. However, the Mediterranean style continues to influence new residential and commercial architecture in the coastal areas of the Gulf of Mexico, Florida and California.

Modern to Contemporary Architecture

(1920-present)

The term Contemporary architecture refers to the current period of design expression. Contemporary architecture is stylistically different from Modern architecture of the early 20th century. Modern architecture abandoned historical architectural styles for sleek designs, devoid of traditional details and became known as the International style. Modern architecture evolved at the turn of the century and flourished from the 1920s through the post-war building boom. Its unadorned simplicity ultimately dominated the design of high rise buildings, but had less influence on residential design in most parts of the country.

In the latter part of the 20th century, trends in Contemporary residential architecture evolved into a number of sub-styles. Postmodernism represents a return to stylized ornamentation. The Postmodern movement began in the U.S. during the 1980s as a rejection of the bland functionality of the Modern and International style of architecture. It is regarded as a return to an eclectic façade design with stylistic references, symbolism and color. Prominent examples of Postmodern architecture are the former AT&T headquarters building in New York (now Sony) and the Las Vegas strip of stylized hotels and casinos mimicking famous structures around the world. "Deconstructivism," another form of Contemporary architecture, tends to distort the shape of a structure into startling non-rectangular forms that may appear to be in a state of deconstruction.

"High-tech" Contemporary residential architecture employs industrial and high-technology design elements that are typical of a factory or industrial facility such as metal stairs or ramps, pipe railings, corrugated metal panels, exposed bar joists and high-tech lighting. These elements combine to create a futuristic style comprised of high performance industrial materials creating unique factory-like interiors that are dramatic, polished, seemingly indestructible and somewhat institutionally austere.

Classic Contemporary architecture is a stylized adaptation of classical architectural forms without excessive detail. Classic Contemporary styling achieves a timeless appearance through the use of the Neoclassical shapes and massing of the structure without the use of dated design details.

Contemporary American residential design also includes a wide spectrum of individual architectural expressions that are not necessarily associated with popular trends. Typical characteristics of Contemporary residential design are large, bold glass openings, clean lines, simple textures, modest ornamentation and use of color.

Although most American residences tend to favor traditional styles, Contemporary design has always captured the imagination of the design profession and a segment of the populous with an artistic penchant for innovative architectural design. Some of the most popular settings for Contemporary residential architecture are waterfront or coastal sites, wooded areas, farms and mountain retreats. These venues offer exciting views that are captured through creative designs, uninhibited by the composition of conventional architectural styling. Contemporary vacation homes are particularly popular as they can provide an exhilarating contrast to traditional living, offering relief from the stress and responsibilities of everyday life.

Creating Rooms

Creating Rooms

Creating beautifully designed rooms in a fine home is the marriage of architecture and interior design. The architecture defines the three-dimensional volume of the room including the design of windows, doors, ceilings, floors, cabinetry and millwork. The interior design creates the décor by artistically combining color, fabrics, furnishings, fixtures, appointments and finish specifications.

This chapter focuses on the design of individual rooms with distinctive character. Creating rooms provides an exceptional opportunity for personal expression or design preferences such as a handsomely appointed library with meticulously crafted cabinetry and millwork or a state-of-the-art "high-tech" playroom with futuristic industrial design components. Some of the most fascinating spaces we have designed are responses to idiosyncratic preferences and concepts for individual rooms.

The design of a room derives its inspiration from a variety of sources. In some cases it is the materials: honey-colored cypress cabinets, herringbone patterned old brick or antique heart pine floors, an elegant arrangement of doors and windows, or a vaulted ceiling with massive wood trusses. Often, a creative shape such as an oval dining room, can be the unique design concept that makes a space memorable. The focal point of a room, like an antique French marble mantle or pairs of arched-top Italian doors opening to a loggia, can become the creative design element that makes a room special.

The design concept for a fine home strategically positions rooms for convenience, gatherings, privacy, proximity to companion spaces and optimal views. Once these relationships are established, creating the character of each room is a fundamental step in the design process. Our clients usually have photographs and magazine pictures featuring creative ideas they want to incorporate into each room of their house. The architect's task is to analyze and incorporate these special features and creatively orchestrate the development of each room in the context of the overall concept for the home.

The size of a room is often determined by designated activities and the number of people it will need to accommodate. For example, the dimensions of a dining room may be determined by the length of a fully extended table and the number of chairs required for family and guests, while the width must consider clearances for furniture placement on the sides of the room. A playroom with a pool table must provide space for the players that does not conflict with the seating area for television viewing, movies or video games.

The kitchen, master bedroom and bathroom are undoubtedly the most challenging and complex areas of residential design. This is because so many components must be incorporated into the design: plumbing fixtures, electrical appliances, cabinetry, ventilation equipment, stone and tile surfaces, closets, dressing rooms and storage areas.

With the demise of the formal living room, the demand for a different kind of space to accommodate a variety of activities has become increasingly more popular. In concept, the great room is an informal gathering place that is often linked to the kitchen and opens to the outdoors. Design opportunities for the great room range from contemporary styling to traditional interiors, from elegant simplicity to opulent splendor and from conventional flat ceilings to immense vaulted spaces. As its name implies, the great room provides grand design opportunities for creating your architectural style.

One of the most fascinating and challenging concepts for the creation of a new room was expressed to me by a client who had purchased a log house on a hillside for a country home. As we reviewed pictures of the existing structure, she asked inquisitively if I could design a large living room addition in the style of the log house. My answer was affirmative. As I pondered how the massing of the new and old structures would unite, she continued with another aspect of the design: "On the inside, I would like the living room to look like a contemporary New York apartment." This is quite a challenging assignment for the creation of a room: log cabin on the outside and a New York apartment on the inside. Years later, I attended a birthday party for a friend and former classmate who had purchased the unique log house with its contemporary interior. Everyone loved the creative design of this country home.

The successful creation of that very special room eventually resulted in an even more challenging assignment when the new owners' home on the Gulf Coast was destroyed by Hurricane Katrina. The creative idea for rooms on the main floor of a massive, new plantation-style home included huge fourteen foot wide windows overlooking the water. Never having seen a precedent for this size window in a plantation home, I cautioned the owner that it might be problematic. He simply smiled and said, "I understand and am confident that you will work it out if you don't want to be embarrassed." He is a great outdoorsman and the vista from his building site extends over a river and miles of marsh. The home is now under construction and we are proud of the design.

The creative concept for a room may be a fundamental element of the overall design for a home, like a central great room with a massive timber truss ceiling or a secluded wine cellar tucked away behind an antique wood door with an iron grill. The concept for a major room may influence the creative approach to designing the entire house, or the style of the house may filter into the creative design of each individual room. In either event, creating extraordinary rooms is what residential design of fine homes is all about. This chapter focuses on major rooms that collectively create the character of a home.

The Kitchen

Without a doubt, the kitchen is the nerve center of the American home. It is the focal point of activity from breakfast in the morning to a snack at midnight. The kitchen is the primary gathering place for family, informal entertaining, eating and socializing.

The kitchen has come a long way since its basic function of food preparation and serving meals. Every family member is influenced by the design of the kitchen. No other area of the house requires as much planning or plays as complex a role in the family lifestyle as the kitchen. Therefore, kitchen design requires more time and thought than any other aspect of the home. Planning the kitchen is like designing a house within a house.

Developing a building program for your kitchen requires a comprehensive overview of the family lifestyle and the daily routine of each family member. Today, the term kitchen encompasses far more than just the cooking area.

To properly plan your family kitchen, it must be considered in the context of the future growth of children and parents. In short, the kitchen must be planned not only for today, but for how it will serve your family in five, ten and twenty years from now. What will your children's ages be in five years and how will you accommodate their friends? Will the demand for informal eating increase during the summer months? How many years will you be discussing homework while working in the kitchen? How will you use the kitchen when the children are grown? These are only a few considerations.

The design configuration of this family home placed the kitchen at the epicenter of the house. As a multifunctional space, this inviting kitchen is a place to congregate while cooking, entertaining and enjoying family activities.

When it comes to casual entertaining at home, not every party starts in the kitchen, but few can remember attending a party without a gathering in the kitchen. As a result, kitchen design now acknowledges its vital role as the center of family interaction.

Since more families today have two working parents, the approach to food preparation and dining at home is changing significantly. Time is a critical factor, influencing not only the selection of foods, but also the manner in which they are prepared. Both parents often arrive home at dinnertime after a long, tiring day. The demand for quick, efficient, time-saving methods of preparing meals is essential. The kitchen must have adequate workspace for two or more people working to prepare a family meal harmoniously.

Family communication peaks at the dinner hour and the kitchen must allow for informal exchanges while dinner is being prepared. The atmosphere should be cheerful, relaxed and convivial while simultaneously serving as a state-of-the-art culinary facility. Integrating a sitting area into the kitchen is one way to foster important family discussions at the dinner hour.

OPPOSING PAGE

Top Left: Large casement windows introduce morning sunlight and provide attractive views of a courtyard, making the kitchen and casual dining area of this home an especially cheerful place. Clean lines and plenty of counter space for food preparation make activities in the kitchen a joyful experience.

Top Right: A heavy timber cathedral ceiling in the kitchen and family room creates a dramatic interior. The vertical height of the space is balanced by the warm tone of the wooden structure. Cabinets in the kitchen coordinate with the light-colored walls and floor. The result is a comfortable, open and spacious appearance. The breakfast bay overlooks a swimming pool and stone terrace.

Bottom Left: Cast stone brackets supporting an antique plaster hood above the stove form the centerpiece of this tailored kitchen.

Bottom Right: Granite countertops, a scored concrete floor and stainless steel appliances combine to create the sophisticated décor of an elegantly simple kitchen design.

Above: The antique breakfast table and chairs in a bay off the kitchen provide a cheerful spot to start the day with windows facing the pool and a door opening to a veranda extending around the house to the front entrance.

The result of this evolution of the American family lifestyle has caused a trend away from functional, institutional kitchen design toward a well-detailed, but comfortable, casual and elegant family area. Kitchen appliances and custom cabinetry available today display design sophistication often equaling the appointments found in the more formal areas of the home.

As the kitchen has developed into a prominent living space, fine materials and appointments have become essential elements of the design. Among these are stone floors and counter tops, custom milled wood cabinetry, elegant fenestration, interesting bays, beamed and vaulted ceilings, imported porcelain tile materials, specialized metal work, creative lighting and exotic equipment.

Top Left: This sleek, brightly lit contemporary kitchen overlooking the Gulf of Mexico features stool seating for casual meals and an adjacent veranda for outdoor dining.

Bottom Left: Neutral cabinet colors and a pickled maple floor create a soothing and inviting atmosphere for cooking and entertaining. A long gray and black granite island provides a contrasting focal point and a convenient surface for serving a large buffet.

Right: A bay-shaped kitchen with custom milled cypress cabinets features a bank of windows providing a panoramic view of the grounds. Antique quarter-sawn heart pine floors in the kitchen, breakfast area and adjoining family room reflect the quality of material selections in this fine home.

Kitchen design today requires comfortable seating areas together with informal dining spaces. Other considerations include a bar, desk and telephone, space for cookbooks, entertainment center with television and music, a walk-in pantry, small appliance compartments for convenient access to equipment, indoor barbecue grills, island work spaces and specialized appliances. Circulation patterns, design of activity areas, placement of appliances, cabinets and windows are other issues to be resolved.

French limestone countertops and porcelain tiles emulating an antique stone floor exemplify the balance between quality and durability in this elegantly appointed kitchen conveniently situated between the great room and family room.

Contemporary lifestyles demand that the kitchen be equipped to satisfy the individual needs of each family member on a daily basis and to provide entertaining space for guests. Kitchen design for fine homes integrates many variables such as: food preparation requirements, appliances, food storage, utensils, informal dining, or stool seating. In addition, special considerations for family needs must be addressed, such as a keeping area with comfortable seating for TV viewing, cabinetry for display of fine china, a fireplace, a butler's pantry, a wine cooler, or high-end commercial cooking equipment.

In response to the demand for more convenient and glamorous kitchens, the manufacturers of appliances and cabinetry have been tireless in creating sophisticated equipment, cabinets and finishes to meet the needs of style-conscious consumers and designers. The proliferation of handsome kitchen cabinetry with built-in appliances now rivals the creations of fine furniture makers. State-of-the-art appliances and exotic fixtures bring new opportunities for creativity in kitchen design.

Rare "sinker cypress", milled from lost logs and tree trunks submerged in rivers and lakes for generations, was selected to fashion the kitchen cabinets for its antique coloration. State-of-the-art fixtures and appliances, including a commercial stove and soapstone sink, make the kitchen as functional as it is attractive. A stairway from the breakfast area leads to a spacious second floor arrangement of children's bedrooms.

As the nerve center of the home, circulation to and from the kitchen is vitally important. The garage is generally close to the kitchen for ease of transporting groceries and household supplies. The informal or family entrance to the house tends to be near the kitchen. The family entrance is the most active point of arrival or departure. This necessitates storing a host of paraphernalia and apparel like coats, umbrellas, hats, boots and other things needed when leaving the home. The size of your family and extent to which these stored items will be needed usually dictates whether to provide a small closet for coats or a larger storage area near the family entrance. For larger families, a mudroom near the kitchen may be the solution.

Linkage between the kitchen and dining room may be accomplished in many ways, each yielding different benefits. This fundamental connection may be a door for direct access or an intermediate space for service to the dining room, often called a butler's pantry. A butler's pantry can be useful for storing china, silver, or serving pieces; it also provides needed counter space to stage the serving of a formal dinner. At the end of a dinner party, or between courses, pantry space is invaluable to retire dishes that are removed from the table. As an added benefit, a butler's pantry provides an acoustic buffer that insulates kitchen sounds and acts as an airlock that inhibits cooking odors.

Top Left: Rich red walls energize the kitchen. A convenient U-shaped arrangement of cabinets with stone countertops also provides shelving for cookbooks. A center island is accessible from four sides for food preparation. Antique pine floors are featured in the kitchen and throughout the main floor of the house.

Bottom Left: Views of a bend in the river are visible through windows at every vantage point in this upstairs kitchen, including the cooking area, island seating and breakfast area.

Right: Herringbone patterned tile covers the wall behind the stainless cooktop, surrounding the hood and providing a beautiful surface texture that is easy to maintain. Matching pantry cabinets and refrigeration equipment balance the composition of the cooking area. At the center of the kitchen, a glass shelf of electrically illuminated candles creates a focal point above the paneled island with marble top and stool seating.

Home entertainment activities require easy access between the kitchen and the family room. This necessitates yet another link to the nerve center of the home. It is also desirable to provide a visual connection between the kitchen and the family room to allow conversation and eliminate the feeling of isolation in the kitchen. Outdoor entertaining on decks and patios can be an adjunct connection to the kitchen. Even the utility room is often placed close to the kitchen for convenient processing of laundry throughout the day.

The location of the kitchen is the primary consideration in planning your home because it is linked to so many other important areas. Kitchen decisions should be determined at the earliest stage of conceptual design. Your kitchen deserves special attention, from the initial conception to the last finishing detail of the plans, to fulfill all of its essential roles.

The Dining Room

The dining room is often the most elegant room in a fine home. When it comes to gracious entertaining, the dining room is almost universally accepted as the place for special occasions. While the traditional living room has gradually faded from new homes, the dining room has endured as an important gathering place for friends and family.

The advent of two-income families with a condensed interval for quality time precipitated the merger of the kitchen, den and breakfast room into a single multipurpose space for food preparation, family gathering and informal meals. As the popular breakfast room has become a larger informal space to accommodate family meals, many homes now feature both formal and informal dining areas.

Despite the evolution of informal dining in the kitchen area, many families still desire a home with an elegant dining room for special occasions. The spectrum for dining room design is as broad as the variety of residential styles.

One of the first and most memorable dining rooms we were engaged to restore was in an historic 1795 French Quarter townhouse inherited by Lindy Boggs, former U.S. Congresswoman who later became Ambassador to the Holy See at the Vatican. Reconstruction of the 200 year-old dining room included restoration of the plaster moldings and woodwork, painting the wall a beautiful shade of red and furnishing it with family antiques. A talented young artist from our firm hand painted a rosette on the ceiling above the chandelier in the national colors. For thirty years this dining room has hosted many cultural, charitable and political functions. The memories created in this room have touched the hearts of thousands of guests.

Left: Walls of glass on both sides of this upstairs dining room overlook a park in one direction and a large central atrium opening to the sky on the opposite side. The dining room has an exciting feeling of floating on air.

Right: Fortuny fabrics, a Persian rug and a wall tapestry surround a mahogany table and antique chairs to create an intimate dining room.

The design appointments and décor of the dining room offer a unique opportunity to express the owner's stylistic preferences. Each element of the design, from the shape of the room to the color of the walls, contributes to the character of the dining environment. More than any other room in the house, the shape of the dining room is influenced by the type of furnishings it is intended to accommodate. While the majority of dining spaces remain rectangular in shape, there are those who prefer more diverse geometric design configurations. We recently completed a new home with a grand oval-shaped dining room including a bow window overlooking the lawn and gardens. The curvilinear interior created a unique space, making the dining experience glamorous and exciting.

Top Left: Venetian mirrors and powder blue walls delicately embrace the crystal chandelier and candelabra of an elegantly appointed dining room in Dallas.

Bottom Left: A French coved ceiling, flowing draperies and views through tall casement windows set the mood for fine dining and delightful conversation in handsomely decorated surroundings.

Right: Silk draperies and a richly patterned ceiling bring warmth and color to the dining room. Lightly pickled maple floors reflect sunlight streaming through tall arched windows of the façade.

When you choose the shape of your dining room you begin to define the type of entertaining experiences that will occur within it. An octagonal or square shaped room can provide interesting interior settings. One virtue of these shapes is they are well-suited to accommodate a round table. King Arthur may have simply wanted to avoid conflict by inviting his knights to sit at the Round Table; however, many hosts find that this arrangement also fosters convivial discussions at dinner and nobody is stranded at the end of a long table, having exhausted conversational topics with the people seated next to them.

In many cases, the shape of the dining room table significantly influences the layout of the dining room. For example, many families planning a new home have already acquired dining room furniture that will become an important part of the interior décor. Therefore, the dining room design must be configured to accommodate the size, shape and dimensional characteristics of each piece of furniture.

Far Left: The grand oval shape of this dining room creates a bow window on the façade of the home. The curving interior walls form a glamorous space for dining and a memorable experience.

Top: Intriguingly lit by windows at each end of the room, a beautifully coordinated soft color palette gives this dining room a gentle warmth and sophistication.

Bottom: Dark ebony floors illuminated by triple windows in a bay surrounded by silk drapery form the setting for an oval dining room table with radial seating for eight.

Other architectural considerations when designing the dining room include potential views and the style of doors and windows, known as fenestration, designed to capture sight lines to prominent outdoor features. If the dining room has an exceptional view of a lake, hillside or garden, how can it be configured to best capture the view? Should the windows be large to provide a bright dining area, or smaller with beautiful draperies to create an intimate dining experience? Careful attention to these considerations can yield a strong interior design concept for the dining room, forming an important expression of your own personal style.

Top Left: A pair of coronation chairs at the head of an Italian trestle table are flanked by side chairs covered with tailored upholstery. The dining room is illuminated by an imported Italian chandelier.

Bottom Left: The glass-enclosed solarium with a black and white marble floor features French doors on the outer walls opening to a private courtyard.

Right: A dramatic plaster cove ceiling surrounds the dining room and emphasizes the shape of the bay windows overlooking the front yard. The deep red color of the draperies, warmth of the antique pine floors and rich luster of the mahogany furniture combine to create an elegant dining room, crowned with a delicate multi-tiered crystal chandelier.

The Great Room

As the name implies, great rooms are impressive spaces. Grand in scale, but casually elegant in style, the great room is designed for comfort and informal entertaining. The great room has evolved in response to changes in lifestyle starting in the baby boom generation. In the decades that followed World War II, American family life adapted to the influence of larger families, demanding schedules, less formal entertaining time, more working mothers and new technology. Coordination and scheduling of family activities became more complicated and gatherings at home were more spontaneous and casual.

Following World War II, demand for a separate television viewing area gave rise to the den, a small informal room usually added to the rear of an older home or incorporated into the layout of a new suburban home. As baby boomers became teenagers, the demand for larger dens fostered the creation of more spacious and luxurious family rooms, often with built-in audio-visual equipment, a wet bar or fireplace. The popularity of using the family room to watch television usurped the traditional living room's function as a gathering place. As formal entertaining in the living room diminished, this space eventually became an unused area of the house. Although there was little or no activity in the living room, it often remained furnished for the formal socializing that was diminishing in popularity.

Concurrent with these changes in family lifestyle and home activities, an extended period of economic prosperity fostered a significant increase in the construction of upscale residences. In many of these new homes, the space previously occupied by a traditional living room was replaced by a library or music room near the entrance foyer. Addressing the need for a larger, more casual entertaining area, the great room evolved as an expansive space with taller ceilings and larger windows, often overlooking an outdoor entertaining area or swimming pool in the rear yard.

Above: A mezzanine level gathering area for children links bedrooms on the second floor and overlooks the Great Room with two seating groups, fireplace and arched windows facing the lake.

Left: An antique French mantle preserved from the original house on this site is a distinctive feature of the new parlor. Wainscoting, a French parquet floor and coffered ceiling provide an elegant setting for antique furnishings, artwork and an elaborate Persian rug.

The great room is often positioned in convenient proximity to the kitchen and adjoining spaces such as an open loggia, solarium, or terrace in the yard. This arrangement creates a nucleus for family activities. Great rooms often include a fireplace surrounded by comfortable seating, large windows and high ceilings with a design pattern, providing scale for the largest room in the house. Ceiling designs range in style from traditional beamed and coffered configurations to dramatic vaulted areas. The expansiveness of the great room provides an unconstrained feeling of freedom and connectivity to social activities in all of the adjoining indoor and outdoor spaces from a barbeque on the terrace to preparing a meal with friends or family in the kitchen.

Top: Oversized insulated windows provide a natural light and views of the landscaped gardens and swimming pool in a contemporary home completely designed for handicap accessibility. The classical floor plan provides interior circulation around a central atrium opening to the living room and a master bedroom suite at the opposite end of the house.

Through the development of multiple seating areas, a great room affords the opportunity for several group conversations to occur simultaneously. The ultimate measure of a successful great room design is the ability to accommodate either a small gathering or a large group with the same degree of comfort. This entails the creation of a sense of scale that is spacious yet personal and elegant in appearance but casual in livability. The great room should be a gracious area for family gatherings and entertaining guests that transcends the rigid formality of a traditional living room or parlor by creating an extraordinary interior space specially crafted to meet the needs of contemporary family lifestyle.

Top: A French-inspired home in Houston was designed to display a collection of objet d'art including Asian jades, Boehm figurines, tapestries and family heirlooms. The heavy timber ceiling, antique French mantel and mahogany paneled doors blend to form impressive surroundings for the owner's artwork and furnishings.

Right: A series of large segmented arched openings extends the full length of the living area, including the dining room behind a sculptural free-standing fireplace. Opposite the arches, a row of graciously draped 10 foot tall windows open to a veranda overlooking the swimming pool, cabana and Bogue Falaya River. The interior décor is comprised of white walls and furnishings in earth tones including comfortable warm brown sofas, a burnished gold coffee table and chairs beside the fireplace that combine these colors.

The Master Bedroom Suite

A truly elegant master bedroom suite requires gracious living quarters, a tranquil resting place and luxurious areas for personal grooming. Each of these elements must be carefully considered in the context of your lifestyle and design preferences. The arrangement in plan and interior décor must reflect your personal style, habits, needs and desired special features.

Privacy is the first requirement for the master bedroom suite. If your home is being designed for a couple, there are several basic privacy issues to address. Consider separating the master suite from other zones of your home, including children's bedrooms, guest quarters, the family room or playroom. Seclusion is needed from neighboring homes, street noise, views from adjacent houses, sounds from an adjacent yard or swimming pools and other undesirable distractions. Finally, for couples who operate on different schedules, a degree of personal privacy for dressing, bathing and sleep can often be important.

Design for privacy requires an analysis of your family's lifestyle and activities. Families with children often require separation of the master suite so the parents do not disturb the children after they have gone to sleep. Conversely, families with adolescents in high school and college sometimes require separation of the master suite so the parents can sleep peacefully while other family members operate on a different schedule. My son once explained to me that he was operating on London time while I was on Central Standard Time, despite the fact that we lived in the same house. Babies are an exception to master bedroom privacy and usually sleep nearby. Since this is a temporary situation, a sitting room or study near the master suite can provide excellent accommodations for a baby and then return to its original use when the child is old enough to move to another bedroom.

Turquoise-color Bahamian shutters and the West Indies architectural style of this new home near a lake create the feeling of being on a tropical island.

Your choice for the proper location for your master bedroom suite should consider present and future development around your home. A minor annoyance from the street or a neighboring property that occurs regularly at an inconvenient time can become a major problem for a homeowner whose master bedroom is in the wrong location.

An unfortunate example of this situation is a couple who built a large plantation-style home with the master bedroom suite next to the side property line of an undeveloped site. Eventually, a new house was constructed next door with its driveway along the side property line close to the master bedroom of the plantation home. The new neighbor's children loved to play basketball in their driveway at 6:30 a.m. So much for sleeping late in the plantation home. Obviously, nobody wants their master bedroom next to a neighbor's driveway. This situation is easily avoided through proper placement of the master suite in a quiet zone of the property.

Luxurious master bedroom suites can be delightful, relaxing spaces significantly adding to the quality of life at home. To achieve this level of comfort, it is important to plan views in all directions from the master bedroom suite. First, evaluate the available sight lines from the master bedroom to the yard and other elements of the plan for your new home. Then, imagine yourself on the outside of the house looking toward the master suite. What do you see? Is the internal privacy compromised? Should the windows and doors be modified to improve privacy?

Top Left: Graceful draperies and Neoclassical columns frame the bay windows and a panoramic view of the gardens behind the master bedroom. Similarly dramatic classical architectural design elements appear on the exterior of this home.

Bottom Left: The interior decor in this master bedroom features a hand crafted iron canopy bed with a chocolate colored coverlet and silk taffeta duvet and curtains. A freestanding fireplace, opposite the entrance to the bath, separates the sleeping area form a gracious sitting room opening to the front porch.

Right: A deck-mounted tub below a pair of semi-circular topped louvered shutters is the focal point of this marble bathroom. A matching marble vanity and dressing table is symmetrically situated on the opposite side of the room. A crystal chandelier at the center of the ceiling lavishly appoints the bathroom.

Sight lines should be analyzed with respect to the timing of adjacent activities. For instance, if the master bedroom overlooks a swimming pool, privacy will not be compromised if the pool is used primarily during the afternoon. However, if you like to sleep late and other family members intend to swim early in the morning, you may want to move the pool away from the master suite.

To arrange components of the master bedroom suite, the first task is to list all the design requirements in terms of physical size and functional arrangement. One pivotal design issue is your dressing routine. Do you prefer a separate dressing room, or do you generally dress in the bedroom, the bathroom, or in a comfortably large closet area? A separate dressing area can be placed next to the bedroom, forming an anteroom to the master bathroom. It is often desirable for the master closets to open directly into the dressing area providing easy access to your wardrobe. Contemporary living quarters normally include separate walk-in closets for husband and wife. The wife's closet is generally one and a half times the size of her husband's. A separate area for the tub and shower is often desirable together with a separate compartment for the toilet.

Top: A freestanding, hand-carved Chinese marble tub is the centerpiece of a new master bathroom in Dallas. A Palladian window behind the bathtub reflects the classical architecture of the home.

Bottom: An outdoor garden wall and fountain add privacy and interest to the sitting area of a master bedroom.

HIS: Perhaps the only thing better than having two sinks in the master bathroom is the luxury of creating two individual master bathrooms. Gray painted walls and cabinets and a marble shower with gray veining give his bathroom a masculine appearance. A frameless glass shower provides a view of live oak trees in the front yard.

HERS: The freshness of the outdoors inspired the design of her bathroom. The glass tiles on the floor are an iridescent blue-green and the ceiling is painted to create the impression of a cloud-filled sky. A Carrera marble vanity near the balcony door overlooks the garden, swimming pool and cabaña.

The bathroom, like the kitchen, used to be starkly utilitarian. Those days are long gone and good riddance. As a general rule, the space occupied by the master bathroom and closet area is equal to or larger than the master bedroom itself. Thus, if the master bedroom measures 15 by 20 feet, it is safe to assume that at least an additional 300 square feet will be typically required to develop a comfortable master bathroom and closet area. Careful attention should be given to the entrance to the master bathroom to ensure privacy if the door remains open. Separate "his" and "her" bathrooms require considerably more space.

Bathroom design ranges from austere contemporary to meticulously embellished traditional. Elaborate fixtures offer exciting comforts such as whirlpool tubs, steam showers, saunas, spas and exercise equipment. The range of materials featured in the bathroom includes the finest custom cabinetry, stone floors and countertops, ceramic and glass tiles of every variety, porcelain and metal tiles and sleek frameless glass shower enclosures. Elegant plumbing fixtures and trim are available in a wide variety of finishes and decorative styles.

The master bedroom should combine the comforts of a relaxed and private place to enjoy a leisurely weekend morning, rest during the day, or to read in the evening. The master bedroom should be arranged in a manner that will present the interior furnishings in the most favorable positions. Sight lines to and from the bedroom should be planned to ensure the proper balance between personal privacy and available exterior views of the yard or grounds.

Left: Oversized windows frame impressive views of the marina from this contemporary master bedroom. Blackout shades operated by remote control provide a secluded atmosphere for sleeping. The platform bed is lit from below to create a soft night light.

Right: Satin walls painted in a brushed silver finish accent the green glass sink and lime-green Italian light fixtures. Glass tiles selected for the floor are accented by larger glass tile used to decorate the walls.

Most people spend about one third of their lives in the master bedroom suite, making its planning and design a priority that will add significantly to your quality of life. Careful design and planning can also alleviate conflicts in spousal routines that often result from differing work schedules, sleep habits and illness, while providing opportunities to relax in the bedroom.

Romance is an integral part of a person's lifestyle and the master bedroom suite is certainly a component of this equation. The opportunity to enjoy an elegant, tranquil and luxurious private part of the home, removed from the demands of other family members, can contribute significantly to happiness and the joy of a romantic relationship.

Top Left: Translucent glass blocks in this master bathroom filter natural light into the room creating dramatic interior illumination. A tub for two affords a view of the bayou and a relaxing respite.

Bottom Left: This master suite is secluded on the third floor with a panoramic view of a southern lake. A celestial ceiling mural features an artistic impression of "the man in the moon" with natural silk fabric covering the bedroom walls.

Right: Sunlight streams in through triple square windows above the marble decked master bathtub. Flanked by matching his and her showers mounted on a marble wall, the projecting tub is the focal point of this spacious contemporary master bathroom. Symmetrically placed vanities on the opposite wall complete the open bathroom plan. A toilet compartment is conveniently tucked away behind the vanities.

The Library, Study and Home Office

When designing a new residence, the addition of a library, study or home office can resolve numerous household problems. Many families are burdened by the seemingly endless accumulation of important documents cluttering the home. There is often no place in the home for adults to work on a computer or projects requiring concentration. Children are continually trying to find supplies to complete homework assignments. There doesn't seem to be any place in the house to complete paperwork, pay bills, do taxes, or read a book. And speaking of books, where can we store them all?

Over the years we have designed home offices to tuck away voluminous paperwork, planned studies for professionals to work at home and even created a residential library for a publisher to display a collection of books. Although these functions of the home office may at first appear to be similar, each requires a different arrangement. Additionally, it is essential to determine the exact type of space needed and where it should be located within the home. While many problems would be resolved by the addition of a library, study or home office, it is important to understand the function of each before deciding which would best serve your particular situation.

Assessing the requirements for a work area at home requires evaluation of the tasks to be performed. Who will be using the space? What combination of work surfaces are needed? Which types of electronic equipment will be installed? How much document storage must be provided? Only after these and other questions have been answered can an informed decision to design a work space be addressed. The intended use of the space will dictate its appropriate size, layout, design and location.

A residential library provides a tranquil environment for reading a book or magazine, studying a report, or writing a letter. The library can also be a writing space, retreat, or a place for a private conversation. Library millwork and cabinetry offer opportunities to create an elegant and unique room through the use of fine woodwork and paneling. While a library or reading room would be a welcome adjunct to the entertaining area of nearly every home, the associated clutter of a home office would probably be unacceptable.

An antique mahogany library table in the study is framed by cypress cabinets and a collection of books and artifacts. The room is flooded with natural daylight through French doors with fan light transoms opening to the front porch. Cypress millwork on the walls and antique heart of pine floors provide warmth through the use of natural materials.

The study is more of an executive office for individual use without the multiplicity of tasks associated with a home office. It is a place to quietly review documents and ponder important business and family decisions. As an example, a study provides a quiet place for an attorney to review a file before a hearing, or a doctor may read a professional journal. A business owner may analyze financial statements at home in the study, or a professor can write an article after class hours. Whatever your occupation, the privacy of a study is essential. The study should be located in a zone of the home removed from the frenetic interaction of family activities.

The rapid, continuous stream of communications and information has redefined the home office. Remarkable advances in communications technology have transformed American work habits and enabled many tasks to be performed at home that previously could only be accomplished at the office.

A home office is usually a utilitarian work area, typically designed to accommodate a computer and office equipment, paperwork, files and office supplies. A home office can provide a dedicated space to review mail, process paperwork and perform computer tasks. A home office may be conveniently situated near the kitchen for monitoring household activities and the garage so documents can be easily transported to and from the car.

The home office also offers a place to organize household activities. Sharing a home office often requires separate work areas to accommodate simultaneous usage and avoid confusion of documents. Working couples who frequently transfer information between their homes and offices are usually monitoring a host of activities via email, remote access to data, video conferencing and

Top Left: A unique oval desk is the centerpiece of a home office at Amelia Island Plantation. Large paned windows provide a stunning view of the marsh and an occasional ship passing through the Intercoastal Waterway.

Bottom Left: The richness of color makes this study warm and cozy. Dark forest green walls, gold framed artwork and a colorfully patterned rug combine to make a comfortable spot for conversation or reading.

Right: The dark stained hardwood floors and matching mantle of the study are completed by a pastel rug, cream colored walls and upholstery. The fireplace, colorful books and artwork complete the tasteful composition of the room.

instant messaging. While a shared home office may be an effective area to process paperwork, phone calls can be disruptive if two people are working on different projects in the same space. The benefits of a shared office space include elimination of fragmented work areas, the centralization of equipment and supplies and the consolidation of paper clutter.

The function and location of the library, study, or home office must be consistent and compatible with surrounding activities. The library is usually an elegantly appointed adjunct to the living and entertaining area that is equally conducive to reading or socializing. A library can be a gracious component of the living and entertaining area; however, a home office in the same location would be a disaster. Likewise, a private study near the master suite can be a tranquil place to work, while placement near the kitchen could be too distracting. Conversely, a home office near the master suite would require unnecessary intrusion into a private section of the home and provide an inconvenient location, remote from the center of family activities.

One special request stands out from an impromptu discussion with a client who said, "I just need a space for myself, maybe a library with a fireplace. I'm the only male in the house. I have a wife and three daughters — even my dog is a female!" This comment, by one of the most dedicated family men I have ever met, reveals the individuality of personal needs. Just as family members need their own bedrooms for privacy, personal care and sleep, each person will also benefit from having a dedicated space to accomplish work tasks at home, a place to study, consider important decisions, or simply find a little solitude after a hectic day.

Top Left: The honey-colored cypress paneling and matching desk in the study are accented by the contrasting grey-green coffered ceiling. A bright bay window creates a reading nook next to the oculus window integrated into the paneled wall design. An antique gilded chandelier and desk lamp reflect the colors of the walls and ceiling.

Bottom Left: A corner fireplace and warm colored walls lined with built-in bookcases create an inviting library in this Westchester County home. An antique desk and a pair of tufted leather sofas provide a comfortable place to read or write.

Right: Reminiscent of Henry Higgins' study in My Fair Lady, a circular wooden staircase forms a sculptural design element providing access to the mezzanine level of the library. A publisher's collection of books is handsomely displayed in oak bookcases completely covering the two-story walls of the library.

Pavilions, Gazebos and Cabañas

A strategically placed outbuilding lends an elegant touch to the visual splendor of a fine home. Whether the structure is a stately pavilion on a baronial estate, or a shaded gazebo in an urban garden, the design can provide a special ambiance for the home. Outbuildings are often among the most fascinating and exquisitely designed structures to grace a residential property or estate.

Outbuildings vary in type, size, scale and usage. The scale of most accessory structures is small in comparison to the main house and often their design reflects the style of the main house or presents a whimsical contrast. Because these structures are intended for relaxation and pleasure, they are sometimes referred to as follies. Some are intimate, such as the gazebo; while others, like the pavilion, can be designed on a much larger scale for concerts, dancing and social functions. Further, while some outbuildings simply provide shelter from the elements, others, such as a greenhouse, are designed for a specific purpose.

As a general rule, a gazebo is a small, freestanding structure covered by a roof to provide shade and basic shelter while remaining open on all sides. Gazebos provide ornamental features in a landscape and a place to rest. They are positioned to capture a particular view.

A pavilion is usually a freestanding outbuilding, situated away from the main residence. Though sometimes small, a pavilion can be much larger than a gazebo. Like gazebos, pavilions possess charm and architectural character and are built for pleasure and relaxation. However, unlike gazebos, pavilions do not necessarily take advantage of a view. A pavilion may also be integrated into the design of a larger building.

Left: Classical design details embellish the façade of a poolside pavilion with game room, party kitchen, bath and dressing room. Three pairs of French doors open into the game room from the porch, combining the spaces to create a large open loggia overlooking the swimming pool.

Top Right: A vaulted porch ceiling supported by a bold truss and paired columns forms a covered sitting area overlooking the Gulf of Mexico in Destin, Florida.

Bottom Right: An outdoor fireplace is the focal point of a poolside cabana with wet bar providing year-round courtyard activities.

Though not technically considered a building, a pergola is a garden structure shading a walkway. Often used as a link between pavilions, the pergola is typically covered with cross beams supported by posts or columns. Vines are trained to grow up the supporting posts to cover the top of the structure with leafy or floral vegetation. An arbor is similar in design to a pergola; however, it is intended to provide a shaded sitting area rather than a passageway.

A cabaña is a shaded open-air outbuilding for lounging and cooking near a pool or garden. When viewed from the main house, a cabaña beside the swimming pool can add interest and an attraction that draws you outside. A free-standing cabaña provides a multi-dimensional aspect to the design of a fine home by creating the feeling of a residential enclave. A cabaña can broaden the variety of family activities and create a stunning visual experience. A cabaña can host a lively gathering or provide serene detachment from everyday activities.

Certain fundamental elements differentiate the types of outbuildings that are appropriate for each style of home. These include the size of the property and terrain, proximity to urban amenities and the array of outdoor activities that can be pursued.

Townhomes are generally built on narrow lots in highly urbanized areas; hence, the residents are more likely to visit a nearby park than participate in outdoor activities at home. Conversely, a large estate situated in a country setting will require more activities on-site. Generally, the larger the property, the more opportunities for a broader range of activities. The more spread out and varied these activities become, the greater the need for a variety of different outbuildings. As a special amenity, the addition of an outbuilding could be just the right finishing touch for a fine home.

Top Left: Delicately fabricated in metal, the design of this inviting garden gazebo includes shaded bench seating cooled by gentle breezes flowing through the open framework.

Bottom Left: Bold elliptical arched windows provide stunning views of the brick terrace leading to the pavilion. Behind the arches, a game room opens to a screen porch on the left side. The right side incorporates a small entry porch, kitchen and full bath.

Right: Designed in the form of a Greek cross, the multi-purpose pavilion functions as a guest house, cabaña and shaded outdoor entertaining area. A loggia sitting area overlooks the swimming pool, lawn and gardens. A cabaña bath and bar open to interior living quarters and the loggia.

Top Left: A contemporary pavilion beside a sunlit pool features post-modern design elements reminiscent of classic architecture.

Bottom Left: An octagonal pavilion facing a croquet court on the front of a Southern Plantation-Style home in Dallas is a focal point in the landscape design.

Top Right: Reflecting the roof design of the main residence, a dormer window streams sunlight into the vaulted ceiling of the shaded lounging area of this cabaña.

Bottom Right: Surrounded by tropical gardens and flagstone terraces, the image of this pavilion is a dreamy reflection on the surface of the immense swimming pool gracefully configured in a symetrical design with raised tropical planting beds forming each of the four corners.

The Wine Cellar

Collecting and aging fine wine is a passion and its pursuit requires a special environment. As the wine collection grows so does the need for space to organize and catalog vintages. When the storage capacity of manufactured wine coolers begins to overflow, or the available display area is insufficient, wine-lovers entertain the prospect of constructing a personal wine cellar.

Wine cellars are as individually distinctive in décor and arrangement as their owners' tastes for the wine itself. Some wine cellars celebrate the aging process with a dimly lit atmosphere characteristic of a secluded underground chamber. Arched masonry ceilings and stone floors can evoke the feeling of a timeless subterranean room below an old castle or manor house. Other cellars are more tailored and structured in the arrangement of wine storage and display racks. Stone or mosaic tile floors, beams and art lighting can enhance the interesting composition of the wine racks.

Building a wine cellar can be as simple as converting an available room or as complex as digging a basement under an existing residence. We designed one cellar that was built within an underutilized study in a French style residence. The height of the room afforded the opportunity to create a groin vaulted ceiling finished with matching antique stucco walls. An ornate hanging chandelier above a rustic tasting table for six provides a country French atmosphere.

Left: A subterranean wine cellar with wood paneled ceiling and colorful glass tile floor is artistically illuminated by perimeter lighting.

Right: A stone floor and groin vaulted ceiling create an old world feeling in a wine tasting room for six. A unique chandelier with candle lights and vines softens the décor that includes antique artifacts from a European winery.

A particularly challenging assignment was the creation of an underground cellar straddling the main exterior support wall between a 100 year-old raised home and new side addition. The engineering design was further complicated by ground water conditions in uptown New Orleans. The structural design was similar to a dry swimming pool with a cast-in-place concrete floor and walls. A heavy steel beam was installed above the middle of the wine room to support the wall between the main house and library addition. A winding stair accessible through a hidden door in the library leads down to the wine cellar. Despite the adverse building conditions the cellar has never leaked, not even during Hurricane Katrina.

A wine cellar sets the mood for enjoying a very special bottle of wine in the ambiance of a room crafted specifically for the purpose of savoring fine wines. Whether a wine tasting venue for connoisseurs or a gathering place for friends to enjoy a memorable evening together, the wine cellar offers an intimate setting for entertaining at home.

Left: An antique cypress bar with triple arched alcoves above a marble counter creates an architectural design element resembling a classical pavilion. Round Ionic colonettes support a rhythmic arcade of casework extending to the ceiling. Reflections in the mirrors seen through the glass shelves give the illusion of looking into a Neoclassical pavilion. A free-standing island with matching cypress panels and brackets provides stool seating. The banquettes at each end of the bar form cozy seating areas below a collection of artwork. The herringbone patterned oak floor is finished to match the color palate of the wine room.

Right: The Roman arched opening in a massive wall forms an impressive entrance to a wine room finished in matching antique stucco. The ambiance of this secluded wine tasting room provides a timeless charm and peaceful anticipation of a pleasurable experience.

Design Elements

Design Elements

Architecture is the elevation of building construction to an art form. Creating an artful structure involves the skillful composition of the design elements that combine to define its presence.

Residential architecture is characterized by a combination of design elements reflecting regional or national styles, responding to geographic conditions, providing light and ventilation, enhancing security, offering protection from the elements and aesthetically embellishing the appearance of the home. The design elements in this section were selected as examples of frequently occurring features that require particular attention to detail.

Each of the design elements featured in your home should be thoughtfully integrated into the architectural fabric so that the whole is greater than the sum of its parts. Design elements should coordinate, thereby avoiding competition between special features. The choice of an architectural style is a pivotal decision because the individual design elements should be compatible with the overall concept for the home.

As a design element, windows and doors affect both the interior and exterior appearance of the home. Some architectural styles feature large windows that ventilate and brightly illuminate interior spaces, while other styles include smaller windows for warmth and weather protection. This feature alone will significantly influence whether your home appears extroverted in relation to its surroundings or introverted with a cozy feeling of security.

Design elements, such as a grand staircase, offer dramatic focal points that often set the standard for an elegantly spacious interior. Fireplace design is another element that has traditionally been the focus of attention in formal living areas. Beautiful fireplace designs cover a broad aesthetic spectrum that is as varied as the styles of architecture. Fine millwork is often considered to be the index of high quality residential construction.

Within the framework of the architectural concept, the collective presentation of the chosen design elements combine to create the overall character of your home.

Porches and Verandas

If a single design element were chosen to characterize Southern architecture, it would probably be a wide porch or veranda. As the indigenous architecture of the agrarian South evolved, the lifestyle and climate of the region strongly influenced the design of homes. Porches became a functional necessity to protect and shade windows and doors from rain and glaring sunlight. These same porches offered a comfortable place to enjoy cool breezes during the hot summer months.

Although the terms porch and veranda are often used interchangeably, by definition all verandas are porches; however, all porches are not verandas. A veranda is usually a large, open porch covered by a roof that extends across the façade of a home and often wraps around one or more sides. Most verandas are partially enclosed by columns and railings providing comfortable seating areas for outdoor living. In contrast, porches are not always covered and usually do not extend beyond one side of the structure. Porches can be designed in a variety of sizes and shapes to address specific uses for access or activities on any side of the home.

Screen porches make outdoor living in a semi-tropical environment comfortable in the evenings, when mosquitoes and gnats become a nuisance. Despite the escape from summer heat offered by interior air-conditioning, the gentle breeze of a ceiling fan on a wide porch or lengthy veranda offers a soothing allure that many find irresistible. The ambiance of a graceful veranda wrapping around the façade of a home creates a timeless design element. The relaxing quality of a porch or veranda can offer a temporary escape from a harried life or a peaceful place to converse with friends. In the north, porches offer shelter from the elements, particularly snow in winter. Porches also provide a covered place to wait before entering or departing a home.

Porch and veranda design employs a wide variety of materials and architectural design elements. The architectural style can be embellished by columns and balustrades. Other millwork appointments include paneled ceilings, shutters and brackets. Material selections for the floor ranging from stone, tile and brick to wood can also complement the design. Geometric wooden frameworks for screened

porches provide elegant design features. Handsome lanterns, light fixtures, fans and hardware distinguish the fine quality construction of a porch or veranda, making it one of the most comfortable and desirable places to experience the simple pleasures of life.

Windows

During my first architectural history class, Dr. Robinson began his lecture, "Today we will concentrate on fenestration. This term describes the exterior openings for light and ventilation that penetrate the outside walls of a building." I thought, "Great! Time for a nap! I don't think I have to worry about holes in the wall!"

Nothing could have been further from the truth. Little did I know how much thought would go into developing each of the alternative window designs for every new home we planned. It is amazing to observe the transformation in a façade design caused by substituting one style of window for another. Picture a typical Georgian façade with a door at the center flanked on either side by two symmetrically placed double-hung windows. Then replace both pairs of windows with a tall window extending from the floor and crowned with an elliptical fan transom. Suddenly, the style of the home has changed dramatically as it appears more French in design. Now change the elliptical transom windows to a semi-circular shape and the character of the façade becomes more Italian. These alternative design opportunities demonstrate the powerful relationship between fenestration and architectural style.

Certain window design characteristics are distinctly associated with particular styles of architecture. For example, casement windows that are hung in pairs and hinged on the sides like doors are typical of both the French and Italian styles. However, if the top of the windows is a semi-circular shape, the styling is considered more Italian. A segmented or flattened arch profile forming the top of the casement windows is a French design, whereas double-hung sash windows opening vertically typify the Georgian and Federal styles. Early American homes in New England often featured small casement windows with leaded glass in a diamond pattern because large glass panes were not available in the new world. In another era, shingle style homes began to appear with an eclectic assortment of window types including the eyebrow window peeking through the wood shingle roof.

While creating charm and character within interior spaces, the arrangement and placement of windows can afford views of the exterior landscape, alleviating the feeling of containment. The proper orientation of windows with respect to movements of the sun and prevailing breezes can avoid heat infiltration and damage from direct sunlight, while allowing cooler air to circulate through the house.

In selecting an architectural style for your home, it is important to explore the implications with respect to potential window design, size and arrangement. The style of windows will strongly influence exterior views and interior design opportunities. Window patterns can frame exterior views and present unique vignettes in the form of artistic designs that complement the interior and excite the eye. This connection to the outdoors is just as important to a successful design of your home as the arrangement of doors and cased openings is to flowing spaces on the interior.

Left: Windows in the foyer, opposite the front door, open to the back porch and brighten the entrance. An ebony stained wood floor contrasts the soft wall color and pastel draperies. Large cased openings on each side of the foyer lead to entertaining areas of the home.

Right: European window designs respond to the architectural style and type of construction. Windows depicted are set in walls constructed of natural brick, wood, stucco over brick and stone. Interesting design elements are created by surrounding windows with patterned brickwork, shutters, jigsaw casework, stone jambs and sill, classical wood trim, or an elaborate stucco cornice with brackets and sculptural relief.

Doors

As a critical design element, doors simultaneously contribute to the interior décor and exterior design of the home. This dual aesthetic responsibility to satisfy interior and exterior design objectives requires careful consideration of the chosen solution for each perimeter door design. For example, some exterior doors are designed to capture views of the surrounding landscape, a garden, pool, or pavilion, while others are intended to provide a handsome and secure entrance.

The correlation between architectural style and door design is a factor that guides the choice of materials, scale, proportions and shape of residential doors. References to French doors, Dutch doors, colonial doors, sliding glass doors or paneled doors connote an association with a certain style of home.

The relationship between door and ceiling heights is critical to the scale of a room. As a general rule, conventional 6'-8" doors are scaled for an eight-foot ceiling. Higher ceilings require taller doors proportionate to the vertical dimensions of the walls. For very high ceilings, twelve feet and above, an eight-foot door with a two-foot transom creates a handsome opening. In earlier decades, tall doors had to be custom milled; however, high quality eight-foot wood doors are now available as a standard product from a number of sources.

Left: A pair of antique doors acquired in Europe by the owners dignify the entrance to the French-style residence. Ornamental ironwork and lanterns enhance the timeless appearance of this new home that replaced a deteriorating house on a magnificent riverside site surrounded by mature moss-covered live oak trees.

Right: The tailored central hallway of this cottage is brightly illuminated by the fan light transom and side lights flanking the front door.

Both interior and exterior doors offer amazing opportunities to unite or separate spaces, not only by the choice of style and materials, but also by arrangement of the plan with respect to other doors. One particularly stunning arrangement of doors connects a series of a dozen rooms overlooking the grounds at Blenheim Palace, built in England for the Duke of Marlborough. The sequence of double doors that joins these rooms along a linear axis is so perfectly aligned that you can look through the first keyhole and see light behind the last keyhole. When the massive paneled doors are opened, the seemingly endless succession of matching cased openings is magnificent. While every home may not be a palace, interesting concepts for door placement can be derived from this example.

Door design signifies the style and character of a home. Paneled doors with arched top rails favor French or Italian styling, depending upon the curvature of the arc. Glass paned French doors with fan shaped transoms provide a timeless design reminiscent of the view from a gracious solarium to a private courtyard. Whether painted, stained or a natural wood finish is applied to a door, its design composition forms an essential element of the residential style.

Left: A series of cypress French doors with rectangular sunburst transoms open to a wide front porch with brick walls and floor giving the home a timeless appearance.

Right: A collage of doorways features arched openings on the top row and rectangular doors on the bottom row. The variety of shapes, styles and colors of these doors, the casework and banding offers an interesting example of design opportunities. Three images depict painted door finishes and three feature stained wood doors. Contrasting wall surfaces in stone, brick, stucco and wood accentuate the door designs.

Staircases

Few design features influence the layout of a two-story home more than the style and placement of the main staircase. Curving staircases add a graceful elegance to the home by softening the rigid geometry of a straight flight of stairs with a linear progression of equally sized treads and risers. Its location can dominate the interior design of the foyer and dictate how the upstairs circulation plan will be arranged. Conversely, a staircase tucked away from the main entrance can offer an opportunity to conserve space in a smaller home.

Having a vision for the staircase is essential from the very beginning of the design process. One fascinating home we designed was modeled after the existing residence owned by the head of a NYSE company. The original house had been featured in Architectural Digest in the 1920s and the ground floor plan was a clever arrangement of octagonal, elliptical and rectangular spaces with a circular staircase hugging the walls of a round stair tower ascending to the second floor. While the owners loved the geometry of the staircase, it was too small for comfort. Much of the house was functionally obsolete – no closets, tiny bathrooms and an antiquated kitchen. With heavy hearts, we decided to demolish the original dwelling with the proviso that the new home retain the same arrangement for entertaining areas and, most importantly, a larger circular staircase. This staircase would rise all the way to the attic level with a skylight in the roof to flood the stairwell with natural light. The result was a stunning expression of the owner's style, featuring the best of the old stair design enhanced in scale and refined detail to create a unique focal point in the new home.

A hand-painted mural depicting swamp scenes covers the curved walls of the stairhall and transitions to clouds as the staircase turns toward guest bedroom suites on the second floor. The ceiling above the stair arcs into a quarter sphere at the turn and continues upward in the form of a barrel vault.

Another story illustrates how staircases can be a unique reflection of the owners' personalities. One memorable curved staircase we designed was the key element of a new home for a publishing family with an extensive collection of books. Our instructions were simple, but the assignment was challenging. The owners handed me a video tape of *My Fair Lady* and said they wanted us to create a two-story library with a mezzanine balcony and circular staircase just like Henry Higgins' library in the movie. We watched the library scenes of Liza Doolittle, Col. Pickering and Professor Higgins so many times we could recite their lines perfectly. We deciphered the library plan from the movie scenes and gauged the interior dimensions by calibrating Rex Harrison's height as he stooped while descending the circular staircase. The library fit perfectly behind the façade of the new Neoclassical plantation style home, with massive Corinthian columns supporting matching porches at the first and second floor level.

Large homes are often planned with two staircases independently serving the formal and informal areas of the house. This separation is particularly important for families to allow children to move easily between a side or rear entrance, their bedrooms and the kitchen area without having to track through the more formal areas of the house. Every mother knows the benefits of this arrangement!

While the planning of a staircase starts with its placement and configuration, the proper selection of parts, materials and finishes are just as important to the design. Wooden balusters or spindles can be fashioned in a wide variety of shapes: round or square; straight or tapered. Iron stair railings offer remarkable design opportunities ranging from curvilinear patterns to straight pickets. As a prominent interior design feature of the home, it is important to coordinate and blend the color of stair finishes with the décor of the adjoining rooms, including flooring materials, walls and trim colors.

Next to the kitchen, beautifully crafted cabinetry in the butler's pantry provides a serving station for the dining room with warming drawers below the counter. Pantry cabinets at each end store serving pieces while glass wall cabinets at the center display fine china and crystal.

Cabinetry for a wet bar discretely conceals wine and spirits while providing easy access to glasses and stemware. An ice maker and storage for mixers are conveniently located in the base cabinets.

Cabinetry and Millwork

Handsomely crafted millwork and cabinetry, often referred to as casework, is a mark of fine quality residential construction. Producing outstanding cabinetry and millwork involves the combination of design, fabrication and installation.

Designs for cabinetry and millwork should reflect the architectural style of the home. The selection of a residential style usually occurs during the initial design phase of the residential planning process, when the schematic floor plans and exterior design drawings are produced. Scaled drawings of the exterior elevations graphically depict designs for exterior fenestration (windows and doors) in a format that must be repeated on drawings of the interior elevations. Interior elevations arc scaled drawings depicting individual vignettes of each wall of a room. Each drawing illustrates the relative size, shape and position of every opening in the wall including doors, windows and cased openings between rooms.

These interior drawings provide the opportunity to design the interior millwork and cabinetry. Millwork design, in the form of trim and moldings, can significantly embellish every opening in the room. Decoratively milled wood panels can define the character of the doors. Windows can be crowned with cornices and augmented with wood panels extending to the floor below, matching the shape of the doors. Paneled jambs, set in cased openings extending through thick walls between adjoining rooms, connote the elegance of high quality construction.

Wainscoting in a library or dining room and paneling on a staircase are also examples of millwork that can provide attractive design elements, enhancing the ambiance of your home. In addition to the aesthetic benefits of this millwork, paneling and wainscoting also protect wall surfaces from being damaged. Other examples of attractive casework include engaged pilasters, a decorative mantelpiece, pediments above doors and windows, bookcases and built-in cabinetry.

Cabinetry is perhaps the most visible form of casework, since millwork elements tend to be applied to walls or integrated into the fabric of the home. Custom-made kitchen cabinets, bookcases, vanity cabinets and closet cabinetry are forms of casework that provide unlimited opportunities for architectural expression and design composition that can be precisely tailored to individual tastes.

The milling and fabrication of casework is an art unto itself. Detailed illustrations, known as shop drawings, are prepared by draftsmen at the mill for use in fabricating and assembling the casework. Prior to commencing production, the architects review and approve shop drawings for accuracy and conformance with the intended design and material specifications. The proper installation of fine millwork and cabinetry requires an experienced crew of skilled trim carpenters, most often employed by the general contractor.

Attention to millwork details is a distinguishing characteristic of fine homes and high quality cabinetry and millwork truly define an elegant home.

Left: Twin mirrors with fixed panels, moldings and cornices conceal recessed medicine cabinets. Matching marble floors and vanity top elegantly appoint the dressing room. Three levels of illumination are provided by the wall sconces, chandelier and recessed fixtures above the vanity bowls to light the dressing room.

Right: Cased openings can be designed in a variety of shapes. The designs depicted feature three different styles – a segmented arched opening with paneled jamb, an elliptical arched opening with paneled jamb, and a rectangular cased opening with inset wet bar.

Fireplaces and Chimneys

Gathering around the fireplace on a nippy winter evening and watching the flames of a glowing fire dance above the logs is a romantic experience. Perhaps this universal appeal explains why so many families choose to incorporate a fireplace in the design of their home. What could be more fun than opening presents in front of a roaring fire on Christmas morning, or snuggling next to the fireplace in a vacation home after a day of snow skiing.

As an interior design element, the fireplace offers a diverse spectrum of stylistic opportunities ranging from elaborate wooden or stone mantels to rustic stacked stone fireplaces with rough-hewn timber mantels. The choice of finishing materials for the fireplace is a principal element of the interior design for every room selected to include this attractive amenity.

Designing a masonry fireplace is a combination of sculpture, science and engineering. As a sculptural element, the scale and proportions of the fireplace create a handsomely imposing design element inside the home. Hidden in the attic, the flue from the fireplace transitions into a chimney and emerges from the roof. Atop the roof, the chimney becomes a design feature that should reflect the style of the home. The intricate and decorative character of European chimneys crowned with terra-cotta pots of varying sizes is a fascinating design element.

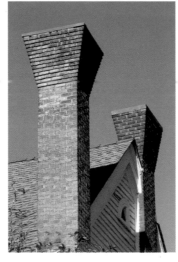

From a scientific standpoint, masonry fireplaces must be carefully configured to provide the proper draft to channel smoke up the flue and draw in fresh air to insure proper combustion. The engineering aspect of fireplace design focuses on foundation support for the heavy masonry firebox and towering chimney. The mass of the masonry firebox must contain the heat of the fire and a tall chimney may require horizontal bracing and lightning protection.

Cost-effective alternative opportunities for fireplace construction include prefabricated metal and concrete systems comprised of standardized components that are assembled on site during construction. With the proper interior embellishment and exterior housing of the flue assembly, one can hardly distinguish a prefab unit.

The outdoor fireplace is becoming increasingly popular as an attractive element of a porch or loggia, or as a freestanding attraction apart from the house. A fireplace can extend the seasonal activity of an outdoor terrace or screened porch and add an exciting dimension to home entertainment and family gatherings.

The majestic and magnetic appeal of fire is a timeless experience that brings excitement, comfort, warmth and beauty to every occasion. The ambiance of a fireplace will enhance the interior design of your home and provide an attractive focal point for socializing with family or friends.

Left: An assortment of chimneys displays the variety of shapes, styles and materials from which these fascinating design elements can be constructed. A cluster of four octagonal brick flues, flared rectangular brick chimneys, an ornate stucco chimney and terra-cotta chimney pots in a faceted design offer appealing rooftop features.

Right: Chimneys are a unique design element in residential construction. The massive masonry chimney of a Second Empire structure towers above a mansard roof and resembles a small classical tower with cornice, dentils and blind arches.

Porticos

As the focal point of the façade, the entrance portico is usually more elaborately detailed than other elements of the front elevation. A stately Neoclassical portico foreshadows the attention to design detail throughout the home in the same fashion that the portico of a log home on a mountain portends the style and quality of workmanship to be expected in the interior. In either case, the design appointments of the portico immediately define the entranceway through the use of refined details ranging from engaged or free standing columns, pilasters, paneling and moldings to rough hewn logs positioned vertically beside the entry to support a rustic canopy.

The primary purpose of the portico is to provide shelter from the elements while a visitor is waiting to enter the home. A portico may appear as a small porch appended to the façade to cover the entrance, or as an open vestibule indented into the front wall of a home.

Left: An elegant French-style portico covers a pair of gently curved mahogany doors below a leaded glass transom that matches the curvilinear shape. Engaged pilasters supporting a bracketed entablature are crowned by an arched pediment.

Right: Characterized by elegant simplicity, a tailored Neoclassical portico with restrained detailing creates a refined entry to a classically appointed new residence.

An entry portico is a tailored alternative to the front porch or veranda that has particular application in urban settings, where yard space is limited or the use of a front porch is impractical. As a side entry, the portico is ideal because clearances are often limited by a driveway or detached garage. The shallow protrusion or recessed design of a portico provides compact shelter at a side entrance and a convenient place to receive packages or deposit rain gear in foul weather.

The exceptional versatility of an entry portico provides the ability to position this design element on the façade or side of a home, as dictated by the floor plan. Portico design has a broad range of applications in numerous architectural styles, providing the opportunity to create a finely-crafted and inviting entrance to your home.

Left: A portico offers both a focal point on the façade defining the front entrance and provides shelter from the sun or rain for visitors awaiting entry to the home. The design configuration of a portico generally relates to the architectural style of the home. These Neoclassical designs feature columns supporting an entablature.

Right: Engaged Corinthian columns supporting a Neoclassical entablature with dentil moldings frame the portico creating a stately entrance to an urban residence. Intricately designed beveled, leaded glass doors and transom coordinate with the acanthus leaf carving on the column capitals to form an elegantly tall entrance. A diamond patterned marble floor and hanging gas lantern accent the handsome millwork.

Ironwork

Few architectural elements rival ironwork for the opportunity to introduce beautiful design patterns to functional components of the home. Stair and balcony railings are perhaps the most commonly fabricated ironwork for residential construction. However, this is just the beginning of the elegant and utilitarian applications for decorative ironwork in the home.

The introduction of a handsome iron gate in the portico of a home to protect the main entrance creates security, while providing the opportunity to leave the front door open for ventilation. An iron-framed canopy, with decorative scrolled brackets supporting a glass or copper shed roof, is a simple but elegant provision for covering a side entrance or French doors opening to a patio. A canopy of this type combines the sturdy construction and attractive delicacy of iron with the functional and efficient characteristics of a shed roof to produce an impressive design detail with a wide range of applications.

Iron posts, pillars, pilasters, fences and columns are forged in a seemingly endless assortment of forms. Cast and wrought iron components provide intricate lacy and curving patterns for grills and panels.

Specialized manufacturers fabricate an extensive assortment of cast iron column capitals and bases, finials, decorative fence parts, medallions, grills, stair railings and balusters. Carefully selecting exactly the right iron components to decorate a fence, gate or staircase can reap stunning rewards.

Far Left: Cast iron cresting, iron porch railings and a wrought iron fence complement classical millwork on the façade of this Garden District home in New Orleans.

Above: One block away, the lacy ironwork of the upstairs gallery on the façade of my grandparent's home is supported by iron columns and covered by a cast iron cornice, cresting and soffit moldings. Much of my childhood was spent in this home and the lessons it taught me about architecture are immeasurable.

The ridge or eave of a roof can be handsomely appointed with a repetitive pattern of cast iron cresting. Iron rods used to support a tall chimney can be formed in a twisted design that is both sturdy and fascinating. Similar iron rods extending diagonally downward on an outside wall can be used to support the roof of a porte-cochere suspended above a side entrance. Accent pieces, such as an iron grill in a wooden gate, can provide old world charm when combined with wrought iron hardware including the latches and strap hinges.

An iron stair railing design must consider the shape of the staircase when developing the ironwork pattern. The more uniform the shape of the staircase, the broader the range of applicable iron railing patterns. Conversely, an irregular stair configuration is more restrictive, limiting the railing design to a simpler pattern. Like stone, ironwork instills a feeling of timeless permanence in the appearance of a home. Elements forged of iron are present in nearly every style of architecture, spanning from classical antiquity to present day contemporary.

Ironwork is an intriguing design element that can be used to embellish the style and character of your home. Whether it is a lacy cast iron balcony railing in the French Quarter of New Orleans or a beautiful wrought iron balustrade in Paris, ironwork is a distinctive mark of fine quality construction.

Top Left: A waterfront balcony railing on a lake in Italy shows its age in the weathered scaling of the wrought iron.

Bottom Left: Stone steps with a delicate iron railing descend to a garden court.

Right: Wrought iron fences with cast iron finials and elaborate window grilles help secure the grounds and residential living quarters with attractive design motifs that add character to the home.

Ceilings

The articulation of the ceiling plain of the American home has evolved essentially as a function of height. As ceiling height increases, so does the human tendency to look upward and admire the design configuration and details. Accordingly, the higher the ceiling, the more attention is focused on the design. Historical solutions to ceiling designs have incorporated dramatic Gothic arches in the form of an inverted "V," semi-circular Roman arches, French coved ceilings and the classical coffered ceiling comprised of a series of recessed square or geometric alcoves each intricately embellished with dentils, medallions, moldings or paintings.

In the cycle of residential building, ceiling height has generally followed the economy. Thus the more affluent the population, the higher the ceiling. The higher the ceiling, the more opportunity for attention to design details.

The current building cycle began after World War II and we have gradually witnessed average residential ceiling heights grow from eight feet in the late 1940s to nine feet in the early 1970s. By the 1980s, ten feet became the standard for upscale residential spaces and by the 21st century, the twelve foot ceilings of the 1920s became a popular attribute of major residences.

As in the past, ceiling décor is commensurate with height and we are presently experiencing a delightful return to decorative ceiling design. Vaulted ceilings, tray ceilings, heavy timber trusses or beams, coffered ceilings and coved ceilings abound in the design of new homes where the height of the room rivals those of past generations.

Roofs

The roof of a home is a design consideration that must be carefully balanced with the massing and configuration of the structure. The choice of a particular roof style strongly influences the design of the home. When choosing an architectural style, it is important to consider that the volumetric shape of the roof can provide bonus space for rooms in the attic.

The massing of the roof is one of the most significant trademarks of a residential architectural style. In colder climates, a steeply pitched hipped roof covered with slate is a typical French-style configuration. A low-pitched hipped roof covered with terra-cotta barrel tile is a more popular style in Italy, where the weather is generally warmer. Georgian style homes often feature roofs with end gables as do Acadian cottages. Adobe homes in New Mexico, Arizona and California often have flat roofs, if they are located in desert areas with little rainfall.

These are just a few examples of the variations in roof design for different styles of residential architecture. Other styles of homes are built with terra-cotta or concrete tile roofs, as seen in Florida. Thatched roofs often appear on tropical homes; wood shake roofs usually adorn shingle style homes; while metal roofs are commonplace on farmhouses. Contemporary homes feature a wide variety of unconventional roof configurations, expanding traditional roof designs to a new dimension.

When selecting a roof style for your new home, it is important to consider the design implications beyond the exterior appearance. Steep roofs on small homes create larger attic cavities, offering the opportunity to incorporate additional spaces such as a playroom, guest bedrooms, a studio, home office or media room at a significantly lower cost than adding to the main floor. However, sprawling one-story homes that are long and wide are better suited to lower pitched roofs because the proportions of a steeply pitched roof would appear awkward.

Roof design can provide architectural character with unmistakable features such as the turret on a Queen Anne-style home. The double-pitched roof of a West Indies-style house, changing slope above a wrap-around veranda or porch, creates the charming appearance of relaxation, while the tailored roof style of a Georgian or Federal home projects a more formal image.

Roof design adds a third dimension to residential architecture that can influence the interior layout as much as the exterior appearance of a home. On many occasions clients have called when their homes were being constructed to express amazement at the size of the attic. This unexpected area has been the catalyst for fulfillment of many dreams such as a huge media room resembling a theater, a music room for the family drummer, or a playroom with accommodations for children's slumber parties.

One of the most successful uses for a large attic occurred when my firm was approached to design a sprawling one-story bedroom addition to an existing residence. After reviewing the owner's concept, which would have consumed much of the yard, I suggested that we construct the new bedrooms and playroom in the attic. When the project was completed, the owner stood in the new triple-window roof dormer overlooking the yard we had saved and exclaimed, "This bedroom has the best view in the house!"

Coordinating the scale and proportions of the roof with the design principles of the chosen architectural style is essential to the aesthetic composition of your home, both in terms of the exterior appearance and utility of the interior space.

A French developer who commissioned my firm to design several homes on a hilltop by the Hudson River told me that American residential design seems to have forgotten the importance of the roof. These photographs illustrate the significance of the roof as a major design element in residential architecture. Important lessons in the composition of exterior design can be learned from historical styles, both domestic and foreign.

Dormer Windows

The basic purpose of a dormer window is to allow light and ventilation to enter occupied spaces within the roof cavity. The incredible variety of dormer window shapes and styles ranges from absolutely exquisite to unbelievably peculiar. Beautiful dormer windows on the roof are just as important to the appearance of a home as the design and arrangement of doors and windows on the walls of the façade. However, the design, shape and sizes of dormers are as varied as the styles of architecture.

Just as the architectural style of a home influences the height, pitch or slope of the roof, it also dictates the appropriate design for dormer windows. For example, French-style homes often feature a steeply pitched roof structure while Italian-style residences typically have a relatively low sloped roof. The design of dormer windows for every style of architecture reflects the geometry of its roof. Italian roofs generally feature a relatively low dormer profile with horizontally grouped window panes below a hipped or shed roof dormer. In contrast, French-style dormer windows are taller with arched tops, rounded windows and ornate curvilinear design details.

Unfortunately, these classic dormer window styles are becoming a lost art in many suburban developments. So much so that one client exclaimed emphatically as we were discussing the façade for her new home, "Oh, and I don't want any of those doghouses on my roof!"

Overcoming objections to dormer windows requires careful attention to scale and proportion. Not only should a dormer be proportionally scaled to the size of the roof, but its window and millwork components should also reflect the same design sensitivity. Casework surrounding the window on the face of the dormer should be carefully designed to embrace the window sashes in the same fashion that the casework surrounding a front entrance relates to the entry door itself. The roof of the dormer should be tailored at the eaves with an overhang that is proportionately scaled to the design and style of the main roof.

Awareness of design opportunities can foster unique solutions. Years ago, my firm designed a master bedroom suite for a young attorney that was constructed within the attic cavity of his existing home. The original gabled roof was pitched toward the front and back of the house without any provision for natural light. The design for the new master bedroom required the incorporation of dormer windows on the roof of the façade to provide light and ventilation. After several discussions about size and placement of the new dormers, I suggested that he drive through town and photograph dormer designs that he found of particular interest. When he returned two weeks later, his first comment was, "I had no idea there were so many different styles!" Needless to say, we spent quite a bit of time making certain that the dormer windows for his home were precisely detailed. As with fine millwork within a home, tastefully designed dormer windows are a telltale sign of architectural quality.

Above: A handsomely designed oculus dormer window and iron cresting decorate the Mansard roof of an historic Second Empire structure.

Below: A Neoclassical dormer window at the edge of the roof adds prominence to the front entrance while providing light and ventilation in an upstairs bedroom.

Three arch-topped dormer windows on the roof balance the massive steps and Doric columns on a porch facing a scenic river. Ridge tiles define the shape of the roof. Guest suites in the attic have stunning views of boats on the river through the dormers.

Swimming Pools

The decision to build a swimming pool is often hailed by every member of the family, although the reasons for the attraction may differ significantly. Young children can enjoy hours of wholesome recreation and entertainment gleefully splashing around at the shallow end of the pool. Teenagers can lounge, sunbathe and play water sports with friends. After swimming, adults can gather by the pool for cocktails or dining with friends and family. A beautifully designed swimming pool presents an exciting venue for home entertainment for all ages, both day and night.

Designs for swimming pools are as varied in scale and unique in configuration as there are styles of architecture. Thoughtful consideration should be given to your family's particular requirements and intended uses for a swimming pool. Long narrow pools offer great opportunities for exercise at home, similar to lap lanes for competitive swimmers. The infinity edged swimming pool with a waterfall feature provides a dramatic design with a seemingly invisible outer boundary. These pools can simultaneously provide the stillness of a reflecting pond and the soothing sound of a waterfall cascading from the pool to a pond below. Incorporating a spa into the pool design provides a relaxing spot for conversation or meditation. For children, a shallow pool with a gently sloped "beach entry" is ideal. For the grown-ups, a submerged bench or shallow ledge may be just the right accoutrement.

We once had an assignment to create a pool that was easily accessible and prominently connected to a long veranda extending the full length of the main house. Perched on a rise above a river running through a small town, this swimming pool was sited on the crown of a 14-acre estate, between the main house and the water. Equally important was the design of a cabaña to be constructed near the pool. The cabaña design took the form of a Greek cross situated beside the pool, providing marvelous views of the water from every vantage point. As a special benefit, the cabaña has an incredible vista across the pool, toward a huge lawn surrounded by live oaks draped with Spanish moss. The design and execution of the swimming pool and cabaña have been a continual delight.

This charming pavilion is situated directly across the pool from the family room and rear porch. The painted brick exterior, slate roof and a large dormer window match the design of the main house. Special features include an outdoor bar, full bath and vaulted ceiling above the sitting area that opens to the yard on three sides.

The design of a swimming pool and plan for landscaping should be coordinated in much the same fashion as the architecture and interior design of a home. Just as the architectural concept and style of the home create the spaces and framework for the interior design, the plan for the swimming pool and terraces provides structure for the landscape design. The swimming pool, terraces, landscaping and gardens should combine with the architecture of the home to provide the ambiance of an outdoor room.

Separated from the main house by a croquet lawn, this swimming pool and party pavilion with guest quarters are each formed in the shape of a stylized Greek cross. The pool has a spa at the end nearest the pavilion. Submerged sunbathing ledges on both sides of the pool adjoin wide steps for ease of access for wading, lounging or swimming. Raised planters at four corners of the pool provide shade and lush tropical vegitation.

Fountains

One of the most intriguing elements to enhance the design of any outdoor space is the introduction of a fountain. The marvelous aspect of a fountain is that it can simultaneously provide sculptural beauty, the majestic motion of falling water and the soothing sound of rain. A fountain can obscure unwanted background noise and provide a handsome focal point on a garden wall, add life to a still pond, or elegantly enhance the center of a courtyard.

A fountain can be as simple as a single spout of water gurgling upward at the center of a birdbath. Tiered fountains are among the most popular, with a water source at the top overflowing downward into successively larger bowls until it reaches a basin at the bottom. Fountain features on a swimming pool often include a series of water spouts spraying horizontally outward from an adjacent wall or planter into the pool. Water jets can convert an entire pool into a fountain by creating a decorative display of gracefully curving streams of water emanating from nozzles at the perimeter.

Natural stone, cast stone and brick are popular materials for the construction of fountains. Stone can be carved to create elegant sculptural and architectural detailing. Carved stone ornamentation and waterspouts provide decorative relief on fountains. Brickwork offers the flexibility to construct wall fountains and basins in a variety of geometric shapes. Cast iron and bronze materials are often used to create the elaborate sculptural elements of a fountain.

Fountains can be created in many forms – from the lavish Apollo and Neptune fountains at the palace of Versailles to a computer-synchronized rhythmic fountain that pulsates to the sound of music. Although most people would not choose these features, they certainly exemplify the variety of sculptural and artistic opportunities that can be employed in fountain design. Whether simple or elaborate, large or small, fountains provide a wonderful combination of peaceful serenity and the relaxing sound of water, creating a delightful experience in your garden.

A glass enclosed second floor solarium was added to this historic French Quarter townhome to view the courtyard fountain and walled gardens. Built in 1795 by an official of the Spanish government and renovated by a U.S. Ambassador 200 years later, this Bourbon Street residence stands as a peaceful and timeless reflection of its history. Solid masonry walls absorb the external sound of excited tourists enjoying the ambiance of the architecture or spirit of the nightlife.

Walls, Fences and Gates

One of my earliest and most vivid childhood memories is climbing on the huge stucco-covered brick wall that surrounded the backyard of my grandmother's Garden District home in New Orleans. This wall seemed to be several times my height and was designed to reflect the construction of the main house. Engaged pilasters protruded periodically from the face of the wall with flat panels between them. The bottom of the fence repeated the offset at the base of the main house, stepping outward to add a feeling of solidity. The wall was banded at the top with a cap that crowned the masonry construction and provided a perfect pathway for me to improve my balance. Inside the wall, the yard was secluded and seemed to be in another world. But from the top of that fence, one could see everything in the neighborhood!

Fences and gates provide a framework for the outdoor space and establish parameters for the landscape design. A handsome fence and entrance gate are design elements that can create an outdoor space by defining its boundaries in much the same way that the walls of a home create the rooms. Fences also provide opportunities to enclose patios, courtyards, swimming pools and yards for privacy, security, or simply to define an outdoor space dedicated to a special purpose.

The introduction of a gate in an opaque fence provides a portal, transitioning from one environment to another, offering a heightened sense of awareness and anticipation. Entering a walled garden can be an exciting adventure after peeking through the iron grille in the gate for a glimpse into a secluded floral enclave.

A granite sill below the gates at the entrance to a Garden District home in New Orleans spans between two cast iron posts elevating the passage above the flagstone sidewalk in front of the house. Low walls below the iron fence retain an elevated lawn and support the massive ornamental ironwork securing the grounds.

Fences and gates can be fabricated in a variety of patterns ranging from simple iron pickets to intricately curving or geometric designs, forming fascinating artistic compositions. Cast iron fence posts are available in numerous shapes and styles to elegantly support fences and gates. Decorative iron finials are cast in coordinating designs to embellish iron pickets including spear heads, fleur-de-lis, arrow heads and lots of uninviting spikes to discourage intruders.

Wood fences and gates provide design opportunities ranging from elaborately carved wooden gates to delicate semi-transparent lattice work. Wood fence supports can be milled in various designs to appear as elegant pilasters or simple square posts integrated into the design of an interestingly patterned picket fence. Wood fences can feature panels between posts, often comprised of painted tongue and groove materials. As a design element, a decorative iron fence, beautifully appointed wood fence or masonry wall can be a handsome addition to your home.

Left: Painted wooden picket fences on the New England seacoast and in the country contrast the rustic four-board fence around a horse pen. Each fence creates a different image and enhances its surroundings.

Right: In contrast to the rural settings on the opposite page, cast iron finials and fence posts combine with decorative wrought iron pickets, rails and scroll work to elegantly enclose the grounds of urban residences.

The Design Team

Architect

Structural Engineer

Interior Designer

Landscape Architect

General Contractor

The Design Team

Designing a fine home requires talent derived from a number of sources. Many beautiful homes are the result of the cooperative efforts of the owner, architect, interior designer, landscape architect and general contractor. The orchestration of these disciplines is the responsibility of the architect who must incorporate the design team decisions into plans and specifications for construction.

The residential design concept developed by the architect is based upon a listing of design requirements provided by the owner that is called the building program. This information generally describes the required spaces, special activity areas, architectural style, design features, preferred materials, finishes, fixtures, appliances and cabinetry. Many clients choose to build a design file by collecting magazine pictures and photographs of selected features to be incorporated in their new home.

When the architectural design concept is translated into schematic design drawings of the floor plans and exterior elevations by the architect and approved by the owner, it is time to focus on developing the interior design. Many owners have an ongoing relationship with an interior designer or have considered engaging a designer who is well suited to address their residential interior. In either event, the owner and architect should begin the process of coordinating architectural and interior design decisions to ensure the proper union of interior design elements and architectural appointments. These design decisions are essential ingredients of the design development phase of planning a new home. Among the design issues to be addressed are furniture arrangements, wall space for furnishings and artwork, cabinetry and fenestration (doors and windows), wall finishes, flooring materials and color selections. A well-coordinated design decision making process involving the owner, architect and interior designer ensures that the plans and specifications properly address all of the functional requirements and aesthetic opportunities that combine to produce an exceptionally fine new residence.

Creatively planning the grounds to present your home in the most attractive setting and outdoor spaces for family fun and entertaining requires the skills of a talented landscape architect. A properly designed landscape plan can add another dimension to the appearance of your new residence. While the architect is responsible for designing the home, an accomplished landscape architect can provide amazing contributions to the setting including designs for planting the grounds, fencing, pools, fountains, patios, arbors, outdoor furnishings, trellises, sculpture and ornamental enhancements to the gardens.

The general contractor's responsibility is to build the home in accordance with the plans and specifications prepared by the architect and engineer, incorporating the finishes, materials, appliances and fixtures often selected with the help of an interior designer. The general contractor must accomplish the intended scope of work and engage all of the necessary trades to complete the construction.

The product of the coordinated efforts of a talented and cooperative residential design team far exceeds the individual efforts of any single discipline. When considering the selection of an architect, structural engineer, interior designer, landscape architect and general contractor it is always important to look for a team player.

The most successful residential designs are the result of the cooperative contributions of a design team comprised of the architect who conceptualizes and orchestrates development of the plans; an interior designer to select and specify interior furnishings; an engineer to design the foundation and structural framing plans; a landscape architect to design the gardens, terraces, planting, fences and hardscape; and an experienced general contractor to command a select group of competent carpenters, workmen and sub-contractors.

The Architect

The design of a fine home is similar in many respects to a symphony. The architect must have the talent to conceive the design as imaginatively as a composer creates a musical composition. This analogy also applies to the execution of the work. Just as the conductor of a symphony orchestra directs the performance of the musicians playing many different instruments, the architect must possess the skill to manage a group of specialized consultants to develop the plans and organize the construction team to build a fine home.

The secret to most successful architectural designs is the formulation of a strong central concept followed by creative articulation of the plans through a series of progressive refinements. The architect must provide the fundamental concept that unites major components of the residence and allows for the integration of additional elements in a harmonious composition. The design concept forms the grand scheme to which all other design decisions must relate. This grand scheme creates the framework, or big picture, that forms the distinctive character of the architecture of your home.

Attention to the technical aspects of the design becomes progressively more important as the plans, construction details and specifications are developed. These design details are the architectural appointments that create the style and embellish the quality of both the interior and exterior of the home. During the construction phase, the architect's technical abilities play a major role in the execution of the work. By carefully observing the work during construction, the architect is responsible for determining that the contractor is building the home in accordance with the plans and specifications to achieve the intended design.

The architect's responsibilities begin with an analysis of the building site to determine the proper placement and orientation of the home with respect to views, sunlight, existing topographical conditions and landscape. Programmatic design requirements provided by the owner are then transformed into a conceptual plan.

Above: The Jack Niklaus Development Corporation appointed George Hopkins to oversee the artistic harmony of the English Turn Golf and Country Club community with sensitivity to landscaping and excellence in architectural design.

Right: Architectural design guidelines for planned communities require special attention to style, site planning, landscaping and use of materials. At Watercolor, the tower of this vacation home provides an observation deck above the roof line capturing expansive views of the surrounding neighborhood and open waters of the Gulf of Mexico. Special efforts were made to preserve the natural vegetation that covered the building site.

A talented architect will artfully create the design for a new residence out of the diverse set of ideas and design requirements presented by the owner. A few seemingly incompatible ideas will invariably appear on the list of desired spaces in a new residence. Overcoming these obstacles is part of the challenging design responsibility of the architect.

An experienced architect can immediately identify the unusual aspects of a client's requirements and utilize these elements to create a special home. By contrast, a less perceptive architect may try to convince the client to compromise their personal ideas for something more conventional.

An accomplished residential architect listens attentively and carefully documents the client's needs until all of their ideas, interests and design objectives are completely understood. Unfortunately, an impetuous architect, who wants to make a design statement for himself, is often too eager to take control of the discussion, leading the client toward the style of home the architect hopes to build.

Over the years it has become increasingly apparent that the initial thoughts expressed by our clients usually identify their most important needs and design objectives. The significance of this observation is that the client will not be able to focus on other design decisions until these fundamental issues are addressed. When the plans have been completed, the architect should confirm that these initial objectives were carefully considered in the final design.

When it comes to developing architectural plans, there is a direct correlation between the time devoted to the design of a new residence and the cost of architectural services. Some residential designers offer discounted fees for simple drawings that can be produced relatively quickly. However, most residential building programs are complicated and it takes a considerable amount of time and talent to create a detailed set of plans and specifications to translate your ideas for a new residence and special requirements into architectural elements of harmony and grace. Fine homes require sensitivity and careful planning to achieve the desired style, scale and proportions.

A poorly designed residence is, at best, a mediocre investment. Remember that the fee to design a new home, like the cost of a real estate commission, is a relatively small percentage of the total project expense. It often costs just as much to build a house with no redeeming architectural value as it does to create a stunning new residence. Time and talent make the difference.

Proficiency in upscale residential design requires a combination of both conceptual and technical design skills. A technically oriented architect usually has a thorough understanding of detailed construction issues. However, designing a home can be a frustrating experience if one tries to start with the technical details and work toward a comprehensive layout. Be cautious not to place the cart before the horse. Starting from the top with a concept and developing a strong central design before addressing subordinated design issues allows the designer to work on various aspects of the plan simultaneously, making modifications and refinements where necessary to ensure that all of the parts fit together within the context of the fundamental design. I have always had an affinity for puzzles and as with a jigsaw puzzle, it is fairly easy to fit parts of the puzzle together in small clusters. By looking at the big picture, completed sections of the puzzle can often be skillfully moved about until they come together harmoniously in the intended composition. This is certainly the case with residential design and spatial composition.

It is important to select an architect who is capable of combining the fundamental elements of your building program into a strong central design. Only this ability to conceive and create the fundamental design will unify the diverse elements that comprise your new home and lead to a truly exceptional design that capitalizes form, function and aesthetics.

A cased opening with paneled jamb between the parlor and family room frames the coffered ceiling and bow window on the façade. An intricate French parquet floor design creates a sophisticated interior pattern.

Two role models significantly influenced my decision to become an architect. At a young age my interest in architecture was sparked by Nathaniel "Buster" Curtis, a family friend and next door neighbor. Buster's illustrious architectural career culminated with the design of the Louisiana Superdome and the buildings he designed fascinated me since early childhood. Another friend and prominent Southern architect, A. Hays Town, devoted much of his amazing career to designing fine homes that combine the use of old materials with new construction. We spent many delightful days designing several fine homes together during the twilight of his remarkable career that extended past his 90th birthday.

I believe that Hays Town and Buster Curtis are outstanding models for all who are interested in practicing architecture. The personal and professional character and talent they possessed are fine examples of the qualities everyone should seek when engaging an architect. They were unusually dedicated professionals who worked tirelessly and were always available to friends, clients and almost anyone interested in fine architecture. Their clients loved them because they, like the great composers of the classical age of music, unselfishly devoted so much of themselves to their practices and brightened their clients' lives with truly artful creations.

Right: Site planning is an essential part of the architect's work. Choosing the proper orientation for a new home and positioning the swimming pool, terrace and guest house pavilion in the most attractive arrangement require careful study. Achieving the best land use plan and synergistic relationship between the architectural and landscape designs is accomplished through cooperative efforts of the design team.

The Structural Engineer

Years ago, my curriculum in Architecture included a course in office practice. To this day valuable information from this course continues to help me avoid problems. The message was simple. "As you enter the practice of architecture each of you will be called upon to provide professional advice. So remember, when you have a problem always seek the advice of a qualified professional." Just as our clients rely on our architectural skills to design beautiful and lasting homes, we always engage the services of qualified engineers to carefully design the foundation and framing plans and ensure the structural integrity of every new home.

Structural engineering is a specialized field requiring specific knowledge about foundation design, the base upon which the superstructure (walls, ceilings, floors and roof) of your home is built. It is often necessary to obtain a geotechnical investigation of sub-soil conditions before the structural engineer can design the foundation. This information, generally called a soil report, provides an analysis of core samples of the ground below the building location. This report determines the bearing capacity of the ground, advising the structural engineer about load limits that can be imposed on the ground before unacceptable settlement will occur. When designing the foundation system, the structural engineer will calculate the weight of the building and utilize data from the soil report to determine the appropriate structural elements, such as pilings, to support the proposed residence.

Engaging a local structural engineer who is familiar with soil conditions in the area that your home will be constructed can help avoid problems with unfamiliar conditions. Local engineers are generally well versed and experienced in addressing special foundation design issues in their region.

The engineer is responsible for designing the foundation and structural framing system for the home. This task entails a review of sub-soil bearing capacity to develop a foundation system to support the weight of the house designed by the architect. The structural framing plans illustrate the size and configuration of wall studs, ceiling joists and roof rafters used to frame the superstructure of your home.

In Westchester County, New York, our primary concern with sub-soil conditions has been conflicts with undetected rock formations below grade and the presence of radon in basement excavations. On the Gulf Coast of Florida, foundations must be designed to withstand the backwash of storm surges that can erode the sand below the structure just as a receding wave washes away the sand below your feet.

Years ago in New Orleans, I asked a veteran structural engineer what he thought about the soil conditions as we stood on an acre of ground near Lake Pontchartrain where we were contemplating building a group of large two and one-half story townhomes. I was surprised when he responded: "You'll be okay, George, if you just don't stand in one place too long." The site, now a major intersection, had once been situated at the edge of Lake Pontchartrain before a major WPA land reclamation project extended new subdivisions half a mile into the lake. Needless to say, we drove lots of piles under the foundation and these large brick residences have never settled – even after Hurricane Katrina.

Structural engineering techniques and building code regulations have dramatically improved foundation design and framing for new residences, particularly in areas that are vulnerable to hurricane force winds and flooding. Thanks to careful planning and capable structural engineering none of the new residences designed by our firm failed when Hurricanes Ivan, Katrina and Rita devastated the coastal area of Florida, Alabama, Mississippi, Louisiana and Texas.

Calls from our clients after the hurricanes provide an interesting perspective on structural stability. In Mississippi, we had designed a two-story carriage house addition that was linked to an existing raised house near the Gulf of Mexico. After Hurricane Katrina the owner called to tell me that his home was destroyed by the storm and reported having shot a 13-foot alligator inside the wreckage after the flood waters receded. He also said that the only part of his house that survived the hurricane was the carriage house we designed with a competent structural engineer. Then he asked if we had ever been engaged to design a large new home as an addition to a relatively small carriage house. This was certainly a first!

In the same region, we had designed a new waterfront home that was similar in appearance to the raised house that was destroyed by the hurricane. This client called to report that the tidal surge from the hurricane had washed through a series of French doors on the façade and out the matching pairs of double doors on the opposite side of the house. Thanks to careful foundation engineering and structural framing design, neither the storm surge of tidal water nor the hurricane force winds had adversely affected the structural interegrity of the home. Unfortunately, the French doors didn't fare as well.

In New Orleans, one of the unfortunate lessons of Hurricane Katrina was that many homes were much better insured against wind damage than for flooding. One client, whose new home flooded during the hurricane, called to tell me that he wished his roof had blown-off because he would have received a better insurance settlement for wind and rain damage than the coverage for flooding. This is the only "complaint" we received for providing soundly engineered homes of sturdy construction.

Top Left: The structural framing plan for a complex vaulted ceiling was developed by the structural engineer to accomplish the architectural design. The shape of the room and absence of exposed beams or trusses required a skillful engineering approach.

Bottom Left: Wood trusses support the vaulted ceiling and roof of a new vacation home on the Gulf Coast of Florida. Special structural provisions were made for resistance to hurricane force winds.

Right: Heavy timber trusses support the rafters of a 25-foot high cathedral ceiling in the great room of a home near Houston Country Club.

The Interior Designer

The best designs are achieved when the owner, the architect and interior designer become creative partners. Talented interior designers play a key role by embellishing the architecture with creative designs, beautiful finishes, elegant draperies, fine furnishings and handsome accessories. Coordination between the architect and interior designer ensures the continuity of concepts and provides for harmonious unification of the design elements.

Before making the decision to build a new home, many of our clients have previously worked with an interior designer. As architects, we respect this relationship and gratefully acknowledge that many of our architectural opportunities have come through thoughtful recommendations by interior designers. The result has been a delightful series of professional relationships, based upon mutual respect, that benefit the clients we both serve.

Interior design responsibilities include the coordination of the color palate blending the ornate Persian Mahrivan rug from the Heriz region of Iran, velvet furniture upholstery and silk draperies in the bow window with the painted walls and millwork of the parlor. Artwork and antique furnishings adorn the room, complemented by a French parquet floor, marble mantle and coffered ceiling painted to match the wainscoting.

Responsibility between the architect and interior designer is generally divided by the building's structural and non-structural elements. The architect is responsible for developing the floor plans, arrangement of interior spaces and the design of the exterior. Important elements of the work addressed by the interior designer include defining and specifying the interior finishes together with refinements and embellishments to the architectural design. The interior designer often participates with the owner and architect in the selection of important interior features such as fireplaces, stair railings, casework, paneling, cabinetry, flooring patterns, lighting for artwork, hardware and special finishes. Talented and resourceful interior designers are invaluable in coordinating paint selections, wall coverings, fabrics, draperies, rugs and furnishings. In order to achieve the intended interior design, it is sometimes necessary for the architect to adjust the arrangement of partition walls, doors, windows, cabinetry, fixtures and appliances.

Left: An elegant herringbone-patterned oak floor in the entrance hall of a French-style home highlights the axis between the living and dining rooms at opposite ends of the façade.

Right: Limestone columns support a triple-ached opening separating the reading room and great room, allowing natural light to flood the interior of an Italian Renaissance-style home.

Top: An elegant dining room furnished with family heirlooms.

Bottom: The renovated living room of a Vieux Carré townhouse in New Orleans.

Top: The colorful living room of a West Indies-style home.

Bottom: The parlor of a U.S. Ambassador's home in the French Quarter.

Top: The living and dining area of a contemporary waterfront condominium.

Bottom: The renovated dressing room of an historic 1795 townhome.

Top: A lofty great room with clerestory windows in a contemporary lakefront home.

Bottom: The informal living area of a U.S. Ambassador's home in Dallas, Texas.

Top: The high-tech game room and bar on the ground floor of a contemporary home.

Bottom: A living and informal dining room that open to a golf course.

Top: A piano graces the living room of a plantation-style home in Dallas, Texas.

Bottom: The dining room of an interior designer's private residence.

Top: Contemporary art and stone finishes create a dramatic master bathroom.

Bottom: A modern sitting area accents a flowing open plan.

Top: A master bedroom with luxurious furnishings in a minimalistic architectural setting.

Bottom: Tall windows and a coved plaster ceiling create a dramatic living room.

Clearly, architectural and interior design responsibilities for residential projects require special cooperation and coordination where the two disciplines meet. This is particularly important in the design of bathrooms and kitchens, where the style of cabinetry and the selection of fixtures are an essential part of the decor. In other areas of the home, cooperative efforts by the architect and interior designer can help the owner make important decisions, ranging from millwork specifications and flooring selections for major entertaining areas to shelving and clothes-hanging arrangements in the master closets.

When it comes to viewing the completed home, the architecture and interior design are inextricably intertwined. Each discipline is completely dependent on the other to graciously and attractively present the creative design concept. A beautifully designed home is most often the result of a successful collaboration by the owner, architect and interior designer.

Top: A graceful, curving arc transitioning from the wall to the ceiling plain creates a cove that dramatically crowns the living room fireplace. Silk draperies with alternating panels of chocolate, cream and lime enhance the tall windows and emphasize the height of the ceiling. Shimmering silk slipcovers on club chairs coordinate with the neutral colors of the walls, rug and furniture fabrics to create a warm and inviting place to gather.

Bottom: In the daytime, the great room is flooded with natural light streaming through French doors opening to a wrap-around veranda on three sides. The cove of an 18-foot high great room ceiling is dramatically illuminated by a series of tiny bulbs, warmly glowing to create a relaxed mood at night.

The Landscape Architect

Developing a landscape design for your home creates the setting for an architectural statement. Natural and man-made elements combine to present the personal style of your residence. Landscape designs enhance the formal elegance of a manor house or cloak a cottage in a charmingly relaxed natural setting. The skillful integration of architecture and landscaping for your new home will create the most attractive appearance.

The art of landscape design includes more than simply arranging plant materials. Whether contemplating the grand scale of a chateau, an English manor house or a small French Quarter courtyard, attention to landscaping fully integrates residential architecture and the outdoor environment. Landscaping encompasses the artful combinations of flowering plants and trees, patios, fencing and walls, fountains, garden ornaments and furniture, walkways and outdoor lighting.

Residential landscape designs may include formal gardens with geometric designs, terraces, landscaped walkways, driveways and parking courts. Other landscape features are swimming pools, spas, trellises and arbors. Flowering trees, shrubs and plants can be combined imaginatively to gracefully enhance the residential setting and grounds of your home.

Left: The repetitive design of this handsome pergola frames the approach to a round fountain from two directions along a garden walkway.

Right: Curvilinear floral designs in a formal garden bordered by manicured hedges form a graceful geometric pattern periodically accented by tall conical planting.

The role of the landscape architect is to analyze the topography of the building site and placement of the residence and review physical characteristics such as natural drainage, contours of the property, sun orientation, existing trees and foliage. If the design involves the construction of a new residence, the landscape architect can provide valuable advice about the positioning of the home and orientation to take best advantage of the natural characteristics of the site and obtain the most favorable views of gardens and landscaped grounds. The landscape architect is also responsible for carefully designing the placement of landscaping and gardens in locations that will foster healthy growth of plant materials.

A talented landscape architect will coordinate design and material selection for planting, terraces, walls, walkways and driveways with the style and color palate of the house. This task is similar to the interior designer's responsibility within the home. Just as an interior designer must recommend durable fabrics and furnishings that are appropriate for the intended use, the landscape architect must specify plant materials that will thrive in a particular climate, sun exposure, soil type and topography. For plants to flourish, landscape architects often provide detailed plans for controlled watering through sub-surface irrigation systems, drainage improvements to discharge excessive rain water and detailed designs for hard surfaces in courtyards, patios and terraces to prevent ponding. Proper design of landscape infrastructure is as important a prerequisite to a successful landscape plan as the proper soil specifications are to each garden bed. If the gardens and grounds are to be illuminated at night, the landscape architect assists in developing a lighting plan to be carefully coordinated with the installation of planting.

Top Left: A tiered octagonal garden and fountain fill and define the inner circle of the entrance court to a riverfront estate. Boxwood lined gardens at the perimeter of the drive lead to the lawn and banks of the river.

Bottom Left: Nestled among the trees and landscaped with indigenous plants, this Georgian-style home evokes a timeless appearance.

Designing and installing a comprehensive landscape plan is similar to constructing the house itself. Such elements as underground piping for irrigation and drainage, fountains, electrical wiring, concrete foundations, masonry work, designs for retaining walls and specifications for outdoor furniture and fixtures are important variables in the landscape design. Hardscape elements such as garden walls, fences, terraces, arbors, trellis work and fountains are vital aspects of the landscape and gardens, just as furnishings of a home are important to the interior design.

Outdoor living areas enhance the livability and character of a home by providing the opportunity to enjoy the grounds as much as the interior spaces. The charm and tranquility of a walled garden, landscaped gazebo, courtyard or veranda affords a peaceful reprieve from the rigors of the day or stress of family responsibilities. Alternatively, outdoor living spaces can provide exhilarating entertainment areas.

Landscape elements can be creatively configured to form outdoor rooms by utilizing shrubbery to define an enclosure with a terrace serving as the floor. An arbor or trellis can be designed to cover an outdoor room with a transparent ceiling adorned with flowering vines. If the sky serves as the ceiling, a constantly changing canopy of clouds, moonlight, stars, or the warmth of sunlight will ensure an enticing variety of outdoor living experiences. The mood of a beautifully landscaped outdoor room can be spiritual at daybreak, vibrant at noon and romantic when the sun sets.

The landscape design for this home created a side entry to the veranda from the guest parking area. The result was a stunning view along the veranda from one end to the other appearing as a classical colonnade vanishing into lush greenery.

From a conceptual standpoint, the owner should first define goals and objectives for use of the grounds surrounding the home. This requires identifying selected outdoor activities ranging from a private garden for meditation to a lawn for sporting. Other popular design elements include landscaped terraces easily accessible from major entertainment areas, swimming pools and spas, outdoor kitchens and seating areas strategically placed to capture a view. These "programmatic requirements" are fundamental to planning the landscape design.

A comprehensive analysis of the property with respect to topography and contours, climatic conditions, soil composition, trees and vegetation, drainage and sun orientation establishes valuable criteria to identify the most appropriate location of each outdoor activity area. These characteristics of the land also strongly influence the layout of a new home. Special consideration must also be given to driveway access to the home and garage, parking accommodations for guests and service vehicles and pedestrian circulation to and from the main house.

Residential landscaping visually embraces a home and marries it to its natural environment, adding a timeless character unattainable through any other source. Landscaping forms the union between nature and buildings that transcends the austerity of inanimate construction and introduces vitality to the design of a home.

Right: The façade of a Georgian-style home is embellished by a seasonal garden creating a lush complement to the Neoclassical entry. The garden flora visible through a bank of windows in the sitting room provides a delightful connection with the outdoors.

The General Contractor

Selecting the right general contractor is crucial to the success of your new home because the construction work must reflect the same care and attention that was given to the design. There are a variety of types of contractors and their methods of operation differ significantly.

Residential building contractors specialize in one or more of the following types of construction: custom-designed homes from architects' plans; speculative homes using draftsmen's plans or a house-planning service; renovation of existing homes; or residential repair work. Therefore, it is most important to pick the right "type" of contractor. Building an exceptional home from the ground up requires an experienced general contractor specializing in new construction with a team of sub-contractors who are equally qualified to produce fine finishes and design detailing. As a general rule, most commercial contractors are not accustomed to working with homeowners. Commercial projects are generally constructed on a rigid schedule and involve different types of finishes. The sub-contractors engaged for this work are often more experienced in addressing code requirements than interior design decisions.

New residences that have been custom-designed by architects are most often constructed by licensed general contractors. These contractors specialize in building new homes designed to address each client's unique personal needs and aesthetic preferences. Accordingly, the general contractor's task of preparing for construction involves the analysis of scores of individual items on the plans prepared by the architect. Before a construction proposal can be presented to the owner, the general contractor must secure bids from sub-contractors addressing every element of the work such as the foundation, structural framing, roofing, plumbing, electrical wiring, drywall, insulation, air-conditioning, painting, flooring, millwork, cabinetry and specialty items. Evaluating and addressing each aspect of work set forth in the construction documents is time consuming and general contractors specializing in custom-designed homes must be thoroughly familiar with a wide variety of materials and services.

Above: Fine craftsmanship is reflected in the construction of a wide front porch at Amelia Island featuring chamfered columns and a square picket railing creating a shaded sitting area. The stone floor and steps provide a durable porch surface complementing the quality of the hanging copper lantern and tongue and groove ceiling material.

Speculative home builders have typically developed standard house plans that are built over and over using the same subcontractors, usually modifying the interior finishes to address customer preferences from house to house. The cost of construction is tightly controlled by the builder, who knows from past experience exactly what materials and services will be needed to produce the house. Stock house plans for speculative homes are generally acquired from draftsmen, plan services, magazines, or plan books.

Renovation contractors are specialists in adapting existing residences. The scope of renovation work generally includes reconfiguring the existing layout by moving walls, changing the use of existing spaces, constructing a new addition or simply changing interior finishes, cabinetry or doors and windows. The construction skills required for renovations and residential additions are highly specialized and this work is quite different from the construction of a new home. Workmen and sub-contractors renovating an existing residence must take special care to protect other areas of the home that are not included in the scope of work. This requires constant care and attention. Though remodeling a house certainly requires an experienced renovation contractor, that same contractor may not be the best suited for building a new home.

Repair contractors specialize in replacing or restoring damaged or failed elements of an existing home. Unforeseen events often create the need for repair work. Some of these unfortunate events include storms, leaks, material deterioration, fire, structural settlement, excessive wear, or functional obsolescence of building components. The limited scope of work addressed by repair contractors differentiates their services from the role of the renovation contractor who coordinates the activities of many sub-contractors, workmen and material suppliers during the remodeling of an existing residence.

Left: Beautiful floors are a hallmark of fine construction. The herringbone patterned oak floor, antique heart pine and running bond brick floors depicted are examples of the finishes general contractors strive to accomplish. Casework, millwork and beamed wood ceilings installed in upscale residences require the efforts of skilled craftsmen engaged by the general contractor.

Private residential construction projects may establish a selective list of pre-qualified contractors, distinguishing them from public projects that require an equal bidding opportunity for all properly licensed and insured general contractors. You should consider inspecting a number of recently constructed homes in your area to identify the relatively small group of residential contractors whose work is outstanding. The architect, acting as your design and construction consultant, should provide valuable information identifying general contractors who are especially qualified and experienced in building fine homes similar in architectural style to the design appointments of your new home.

However, your personal relationship with the contractor is the ultimate test of suitability. Upscale residential contractors are best qualified to address our clients' needs, both from the standpoint of "TLC" and performance during construction. The process for making design decisions for fine homes often extends into the construction phase. Accommodating this process often requires patience on the part of the general contractor. In this regard, our limited experience with commercial contractors addressing residential construction has been difficult at best and generally unsatisfactory when compared to the work of residential contractors.

If you intend to obtain competitive bids for construction, it is important to solicit construction proposals from several residential general contractors. In addition to your architect, other good sources for identifying qualified contractors are friends who have recently completed similar residential projects and suppliers of upscale materials, cabinetry, millwork and windows. Every region has exceptionally qualified general contractors with the required experience to build fine homes. You will be pleasantly surprised to find that the names of general contractors will begin to recur as your search continues. Inquire about the best workmanship rather than the best price and you will quickly find the most qualified contractors.

Above: Beautifully crafted millwork is a hallmark of fine homebuilding. These French doors, side lights and fan window transom were custom milled from antique cypress material acquired by the owner.

With the assistance of the architect, narrow the field of potential general contractors to a few bidders based upon the required skills to build your new home and compatible personalities that will ensure the ability to work together. Provide each general contractor with a complete set of plans and request that construction proposals be submitted to the architect by a required deadline — usually four to six weeks to allow time for the contractors to obtain sub-contractual bids, evaluate project costs and prepare proposals to build your home.

In summary, when planning to build a new home it is vitally important to select a general contractor who has the proper experience and approach to building that will ensure the successful completion of your new home. In this regard, the best approach to identifying qualified residential contractors is to inspect their work and check references, particularly customers living in new homes built by the general contractor. The final decision to hire a general contractor should also carefully consider your personal compatibility and your confidence that the contractor will be accessible, committed to your project and accommodating in the resolution of complex building issues. Under the best of circumstances, you will encounter unanticipated issues and difficult decisions to be addressed while building your home. Be certain that you and your contractor can manage them productively.

Kitchens are the most complicated aspect of new home construction. The general contractor must be thoroughly knowledgeable about materials and methods of installation for everything from granite countertops and range hood ventilation to plumbing connections and cabinetry. Experience is a prerequisite for extraordinary performance in upscale residential construction.

Glossary

ACADIAN PLANTATIONS

The Acadian style of the mid-to-late 1700s is the most primitive type of plantation.

The ground level of the Acadian Plantation is usually constructed of brick or stone and the upper levels are typically framed in wood and covered with an exterior wood siding. The roof structure is steeply pitched with end gables and windows on the sides of the house allowing for light and fresh air to penetrate the attic level. The front roof structure rests on the thick walls that enclose the main floor and on a row of front porch columns. The roof overhanging the front porch is supported by wooden columns at the main floor level and brick piers on the ground floor level. The front staircase to the exterior gallery provides the only circulation between levels of the home.

The windows were very simple because these structures were the earliest style of plantation. Doors, like the windows, were surrounded with simple, wooden casings. Each of the double-hung window sashes was comprised of 8 or 12 small panes.

ACANTHUS

An herb plant of the Mediterranean region whose stylized leaves form the decorative motif on column capitals of the Corinthian and Composite Orders and elements of classical architecture.

ADOBE BRICK

Large, handmade, roughly molded, sun-dried clay bricks of varying sizes used by the Spanish for building in the Southwest.

AESTHETICS

The nature of art and the philosophical criteria for artistic judgment.

ANTEBELLUM

Before the Civil War in America.

ANTEROOM

A room adjacent to a principal space that serves as a waiting area preceding entry into the more important room.

ARBOR

An independent garden structure forming an open wooden or metal framework that is usually covered with plants or vines.

ARCHITRAVE

The lowest of the three main components of a classical Greek or Roman entablature.

ASYMMETRICAL

A composition of elements that is not arranged identically about a central axis; a disproportionate configuration.

ATRIUM

A court or central courtyard open vertically to the sky and surrounded by an arcade or colonnaded walk.

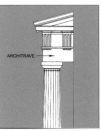

ATTIC

The space within the pitched roof of a house.

$\mathcal{B}$

BALCONY

A projecting platform on the exterior wall of a building that is usually enclosed by a railing or balustrade. Balconies are either cantilevered outward from the exterior wall or supported from below by columns or brackets.

BALUSTER

A number of short vertical spindles or pickets supporting the handrail of a stair or balcony.

BALUSTRADE

A complete railing system including an assembly of balusters, top and bottom railings, and banister along the edge of a balcony, stair or on a terrace.

BAND

A continuous flat horizontal member, series of moldings, or fascia projecting slightly from the face of a wall, thereby dividing the wall surface or surrounding a building.

BARGEBOARD

A wide flat plank used in the construction of thin walls in houses, sheds and barns, also used for fences and on the projecting eave of a gable roof.

BAROQUE

A grandiose and lavish style of architecture that is characterized by exuberant decoration and expansive curvilinear forms in complex compositions. The Baroque style originated in Italy and spread throughout Europe in the 1600s.

BARREL TILE

A clay roof tile shaped like a half cylinder.

BARREL VAULT

An elongated, semi-circular vault shaped like a half cylinder supported by an arcade, a pair of parallel walls or a colonnade that intersects the bottom edges of the vault.

BAS-RELIEF

A cast or carved design projecting in low profile above a flat background surface.

BATTEN SHUTTERS

Narrow strips of wood that cover the joint between vertical boards in the same plane.

BAYS

Repetitive sections of a building. A window projecting outward beyond an exterior wall plane. The space or interval between two or more columns or piers.

BEADED BOARD

Finished wood material with a rounded detail milled along the edge of the outer surface that is separated from the remaining face of the board by a shallow groove.

BELT COURSES

A horizontal masonry band on the exterior of a building that usually corresponds with the edge of an interior floor. Also known as a string course, this band serves to shed water from the wall.

BLINDS

An assembly of slats, a shade or a screen to obstruct vision or block light.

BRICK MASONRY

A method of constructing walls using bricks bonded together by mortar.

BEAM

A structural framing member spanning horizontally.

BELVEDERE

A small rooftop pavilion from which to observe a view.

BOUSILLAGE

A method of constructing walls using a mixture of mud and moss as infill between heavy timber posts, beams and braces.

BRICK PIERS

A series of short columns composed of solid brick masonry used to elevate the floor level of a building. The mass of solid brick masonry that supports an arch or occurs between doors, windows or other openings.

BEAUX ARTS

A classical style of French architecture embodying the design principles established by the Ecole des Beaux Arts in Paris. Public buildings and private residences of this style feature classically symmetrical façades, monumental staircases, rusticated ground floor walls and stone arches, balustrades, quions, swags, and extravagant detailing.

BEVELED GLASS

A sheet of glass, glass pane or decorative glass element with tapered edges.

BRACKET

A strut or angled support attached to a wall to provide structural or visual support below a balcony, overhang, projecting roof or cornice.

BRICK VENEER

An exterior wall surface made of brick that is attached to an interior wall constructed of another material, usually wood framing or concrete block.

BRIQUETTE ENTRE POTEAUX

A method of wall construction utilizing brick infill between heavy timber posts and diagonal wooden bracing.

BUILDING COMPONENTS

Components used in the construction of buildings such as wood, steel, concrete, brick, tile, mortar, and glass.

BUTTRESS

One of a series of external masonry projections from an outside wall of a structure designed to resist lateral forces pushing outward from the weight of the roof or interior vaulting.

C

CABAÑA

A Spanish term for an open structure or bathhouse providing shelter near a beach or swimming pool.

CAMPANILE

The Italian word for a freestanding bell tower usually detached from the main body of a church or building.

CAPE COD STYLE

Cape Cod-style homes (1600-1800) are thought to have been the first permanent houses built in the New World. Original Cape Cod homes constructed in Massachusetts are strictly rectangular volumes that are comprised of one and a half stories with a symmetrical arrangement of windows about the front door. Typically, there are two windows on either side of the front entrance. Cape Cod houses generally have a central chimney with four rooms arranged around it on the ground floor and two smaller rooms within the roof structure. The massive central chimney is usually built of brick, however, stone is occasionally used. The roof structure of a Cape Cod cottage is generally a steeply pitched gable, however, gambrel roof structures also occur on this style of home. Exterior walls are generally crafted of wood shingles or clapboards. Double-hung windows are simple and can be comprised of as many as twenty small panes of glass. Dormer windows in the roof can be used to provide light and ventilation in the attic rooms. Cape Cod cottages are almost always constructed of wood siding or weathered shingles for the exterior walls. The main entrance to the Cape Cod cottage is a simple wooden door that often has some type of detailed relief, such as paneling. The windows are double hung with both equal-sized sashes divided into numerous smaller panes. Door and window casings consist of simple wooden trim with very little detailing.

CARPORT

A covered area with open sides providing shelter for one or more automobiles.

CARTOUCHE

An ornamental architectural element in the form of an oval or scroll-shaped tablet bearing an inscription and often decorated with garlands or swags in bas-relief.

CASEMENTS WINDOWS

Operable windows usually matching the full size of the opening and hinged at the side of the window jamb to swing open into or outside of a room like a door.

CASING

Flat or molded trim around a door or window opening or finished woodwork of uniform profile used to cover or obscure a post or beam.

CAST IRON

Molded iron shapes used for ornamental architectural appointments on columns, railings, fences and decorative features on buildings.

CHAIN WALL

The component of a foundation system used to raise the structure above the ground. A low wall running continuously around the perimeter of a structure and gridded below the interior area to provide foundation support.

CHIMNEY

A vertical non-combustible shaft or structure rising above the roof and having one or more flues to carry smoke from fireplaces away from the building.

CLAPBOARDS

Exterior wood siding comprised of overlapping horizontal boards that are commonly used to cover the outside of a wood frame structure. Clapboards are wedge shaped in section with the upper edge being thinner than the lower edge. This type of siding is also known as weatherboards.

CLASSIC ARCHITECTURE

Pertaining to the architectural style of ancient Greece or Rome or to the subsequent styles that evolved from these building types. The architecture of ancient Greece and Rome was comprised of five orders: Doric, Ionic, Corinthian, Tuscan, and Composite.

CLAY TILES

Thin, flat clay or ceramic surfacing units, having either a glazed or unglazed wearing surface, that are used for flooring, roofing and other building purposes.

COFFERED CEILING

A ceiling comprised of a series of recessed panels formed in a geometric pattern elaborately decorated with moldings or cast plaster ornamentation.

COLOMBAGE

A structural framework comprised of upright wooden timbers with gaps between filled with torchis (a mix of manure, straw and clay).

COLONIAL ARCHITECTURE

Early colonial settlers (1600-1780) initially designed and constructed their new homes in a style that closely resembled their previous houses in Europe. The term "Colonial" alone generally refers to English colonial architecture. The terms "French," "Spanish," "Dutch" and "English" are often used to differentiate and classify colonial architecture based upon the design characteristics that early settlers imported from their native homelands. Thick adobe brick walls and low-pitched or flat roofs usually characterize Spanish colonial architecture. French colonial houses are more often timber framed with high-pitched roofs. Conventional building materials were scarce in the colonies making deviations from the former European designs inevitable. As an example, steep English roofs were replaced by lower pitched structures when it was determined that thatched roofing material performed poorly on homes in the new world. Split shingles, or "shakes," that do not require a steep pitch to shed water, replaced thatched roofs.

COLONIAL REVIVAL ARCHITECTURE

Colonial architecture fell out of favor with architects and builders after the American Revolution in 1776. The centennial exposition in Philadelphia in 1876 was the event that spawned the Colonial Revival style of architecture (1880-1940). The Colonial Revival typically refers to the rebirth of interest in the English and Dutch colonial styles, however, the Georgian and the Federal styles of residential architecture are also major components of this revival period. Colonial Revival homes tend to be combinations of detailing imitated from the Georgian, Federal, and Colonial styles. Colonial Revival houses also tend to be more detailed with ornament, whereas the original colonial homes were generally rather simple. Classical ornamentation such as decorative cornices and classically ordered columns are frequently, but sparingly, used on Colonial Revival homes. The facades are usually flat and symmetrical. Colonial Revival homes feature gabled, hipped, or gambrel roofs. Like the Federal style, Colonial Revival houses often feature a small pedimented portico supported by columns or pilasters to enhance the main entrance. Colonial Revival windows are double hung with upper sashes typically divided into multiple panes. The lower sash of these windows usually has a single pane of glass. Exterior shutters are a common feature on Colonial Revival windows.

COLONNADE

A row of columns situated at regular intervals and aligned in a straight or arced pattern to support a beam, entablature or series of arches.

COLONNETTE

Slender round wooden columns that are milled (turned) on a lathe.

COLUMN

A vertical structural member that is generally either round, square or rectangular in shape. Classical columns are usually comprised of a base, shaft and capital.

CONTEMPORARY STYLE

Classic contemporary architecture is a stylized adaptation of classical architectural forms, devoid of excessive detail. Contemporary trends also include postmodernism, a return to stylized ornamentation, and "deconstructivism" that tends to distort the shape of a structure into startling non-rectangular forms that may appear to be in a state of deconstruction. High-tech architecture features industrial materials used to create unique homes. In contrast, organic architecture is comprised of fluid curvilinear shapes found in the natural environment.

CORINTHIAN COLUMN

A style of the classical order of columns generally having a fluted shaft and an inverted bell shaped capital. Eight acanthus leaves on the face of the capital support four projecting volutes.

CORINTHIAN ORDER

The most elegant and ornamentally detailed of the three orders of columns developed by the Greeks. The Corinthian column has a tall base, pedestal, slender fluted shaft, fillets, ornate capital with carved acanthus leaves and an elaborate cornice.

CORNICE

The upper portion of a classical entablature. A projecting ornamental molding along the top of a building, wall, pillar or eave of a roof. Exterior trim located where a wall and roof intersect including the soffit, fascia and crown molding.

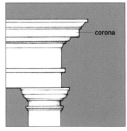

CORONA

The horizontal member of a classical entablature immediately below the crown molding and projecting from the cornice above the bed molding.

COTTAGE

A small, rustic country house usually having weatherboard (clapboard) siding, wooden columns and an asymmetrical plan.

COURTYARD

An open outdoor area surrounded by buildings and walls, concealed from public view and serving as a private or semipublic space often including gardens or landscaping.

CREOLE COTTAGE

A style of cottages in New Orleans constructed during the post-colonial period.

CRENELLATION

A form of notch-shaped fortification at the top of a castle wall consisting of alternating solid segments known as merlons and openings called crenels.

CRESTING

Architectural ornamentation atop the uppermost element of a building.

CROSS VENTILATION

The natural movement of air through a building designed and oriented to facilitate fresh air entering the structure on one side and exiting on the opposite side. This method of ventilation depends upon prevailing breezes to reduce interior temperatures.

CROWN

The uppermost element of an architectural feature including the key of an arch or the upper molding of a cornice.

CRUCIFORM

The cross-shaped plan of a large church formed by the intersection of the transepts (side wings) extending outward from the linearly aligned nave (seating area), chancel (choir) and apse (alter).

CUPOLA

A small towering architectural element rising from the roof, usually having a dome or turret above a louvered or glazed shaft. A cupola is usually polygonal in shape and mounted above the roof on a base of similar configuration.

DÈCOR

The combination of finishes, fabrics, rugs, fixtures, furnishings and objects of art used in interior decoration to create an atmosphere or style.

DENTILS

A series of small rectangular blocks resembling teeth that are placed in a row to form a part of a classical cornice in Roman and Greek architecture.

DETAIL
A small subordinated feature of a building, painting, statue or work of art that can be observed as an individual design element.

DETAILED RELIEF
Embossed or carved decorative forms or figures that are raised above the background plane.

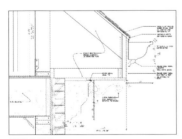

DETAILING
The process of developing design drawings for the purpose of visually illustrating the manner in which a design element is to be formed.

DIMENSIONAL LUMBER
Lumber milled to specific uniform sizes.

DORIC ORDER
A classical Greek order of columns noted for its simplicity and distinguished by the absence of a base and unadorned capital.

DORMER
A small gable projecting from a sloping roof forming a small structure on top of the roof that usually houses a vertical window or louvered vent providing light or attic ventilation. The name was derived from the French term "to sleep" as dormers usually served as sleeping quarters.

DOUBLE DOORS
Two matching vertical doors installed within the same opening, hinged on opposite sides of the jamb, meeting in the middle of the opening, and swinging in the same direction. Also referred to as French doors.

DOUBLE-HUNG WINDOW
A window system comprised of two sashes sliding vertically in separate tracks opening the upper and lower parts of the window. Each sash is often counterbalanced with weights and pulleys (or springs) to ease opening and closing.

DUTCH COLONIAL ARCHITECTURE
Dutch control of the colonies in the New World was brief, however, it had a significant impact on the design of houses built at the time. Early examples of this architectural style (1625-1800) had sim-

ple masonry walls of stone and gable roofs. A gambrel roof is the most distinctly Dutch feature of this colonial style residence. These uniquely shaped roofs have four sides and stand rather tall. Often, the eaves flare at the bottom and deeply overhang the rest of the structure. Gambrel roofs were more often built in the countryside. The more formal Dutch colonial architecture in towns frequently was comprised of buildings with simple gabled roofs and heavy stone end walls overlapping the roof to form a parapet incorporating two massive chimneys at either end of the building. Dutch colonial houses were built in a rambling style, as new living spaces were needed. Exterior doors of a Dutch colonial-style house were often divided horizontally into upper and lower panels that would open separately, so as to allow fresh air to enter the home while keeping farm animals out. The original Dutch colonial residences featured double windows with two levels of glass stacked, one atop the other.

DUTCH DOOR
A door consisting of two independent leaves placed in a single opening, one situated directly above the other, and hinged so that the leaves may be operated separately or together.

EAVE

The underpart of a projecting overhang at the lower edge of a sloping roof that extends beyond the face of the wall below.

ECCENTRIC

A deviating condition or design feature that is off center or does not have the same center or center line as other elements.

ECLECTIC

An edifice comprised of architectural elements from diverse styles or interior design features that originated in a variety of historic periods and geographic areas.

ECLECTIC STYLE PLANTATIONS

Some plantation homes cannot be classified in one particular category and are, therefore, considered to be an eclectic mixture of different styles. These houses typically include eccentric and ornate detailing that is not often used on this type of building. San Francisco Plantation in Reserve, Louisiana is one of the best examples of this unique style because it is an interesting combination of the Gothic, Classic, and Victorian architectural elements. Two more examples of Eclectic-style plantations appear along the Mississippi riverfront near New Orleans. The Steamboat houses, as they are known, exhibit interesting detailing, including thin columns on the gallery level with railings between them that are draped with double strands of wooden "pearls." The detailing of Eclectic Style Plantations homes is remarkably eccentric. Railings at the gallery level are often an intricate pattern made of ironwork. Eclectic-style plantations often feature

two levels of smaller columns or pilasters instead of the large classical Greek Revival columns. A belvedere or widows walk atop the roof is a very common feature of Eclectic-style plantation homes. Italianate brackets are also a common decorative element. Windows of Eclectic-style plantations are very detailed and ornate. French doors are often used in lieu of windows. Shutters generally accompany all window and door openings. Ornate dormer windows commonly decorate the moderately pitched roof structure of the Eclectic-style plantation home.

EGG AND DART

A classic decorative molding design pattern of alternating shapes forming a series of vertical oval formed elements separated by grooves and raised rims.

ELLIPTICAL

A figure resembling a full or partial ellipse with a radius of curvature that is continually changing. As an example, a three-centered arch forming an elliptical curve.

EMBELLISHMENT

Adornment with decorative elements and architectural ornamentation.

ENGAGED PILASTER

A decorative, shallow, non-structural column or pillar attached to and projecting outward from a wall surface.

ENGLISH COLONIAL ARCHITECTURE

The English colonial houses built following the initial settlement of North America were generally late medieval structures. This was the only architectural style found in the colonies until around 1700 when Georgian architecture was first introduced. The major distinguishing characteristic that makes post-medieval English houses colonial, and not Georgian, is a lack of ornamentation. Windows were small with fixed glass and chimneys were very large to generate and retain heat. English colonial homes originally had steeply pitched, side-gabled roofs. However, roof pitches became lower with the use of wood shakes. Sizeable chimneys made of solid masonry were either centrally located or situated at one end of the building. Windows were small with diamond-shaped glass panes that were fixed in place. English colonial homes were typically symmetrical in plan and one room deep. In the northern colonies, timber framing was covered with wood shingles to form walls on two-story houses. Houses in the southern colonies typically were one-story brick buildings. English colonial houses were rarely painted. The front door was typically composed of vertically joined wooden boards with little or no decoration. Decorative moldings were rarely used on windows and doors.

ENTABLATURE
The upper part of a classical order consisting of the architrave, frieze and cornice that combine to form a base for the pediment. The entablature is supported by columns and has proportions and detailing that are different for each of the classical orders.

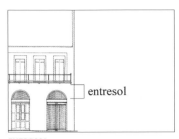

ENTRESOL
An intermediate level in Spanish Colonial architecture for storage between the ground floor and upper floor of a house.

ETCHED GLASS
Glass with a design on the surface that is produced by an application of acid or through a process of sand blasting.

EYEBROW DORMER WINDOW
A dormer window that is elongated horizontally with a low, curvilinear roof shaped like an upper eyelid.

FAÇADE
The front exterior elevation or principal face of a building containing the entrance and characterized by stylistic design details.

FANLIGHT
A half-round, oval or elliptical transom above a door or window having radiating fan-shaped muntins.

FARMHOUSE
A style of rural home first built for the owners or residents of a country property or agricultural land.

FASCIA
A flat horizontal board, band belt or molding on the surface of a wall or covering the ends of roof rafters.

FAUBOURG
A French term for a suburb of a city.

FEDERAL ARCHITECTURE

The Federal style (1780-1820) was an American adaptation of the popular English architecture designed by Robert and James Adam during the late 18th and early 19th centuries. It was called the Federal style in America because of its popularity with the leaders of the new nation. The Federal style featured graceful proportions and elegant simplicity similar to the Georgian-style, but it is distinct and unique in many ways. Federal architecture tends to have more delicate and refined decorative elements than the detailing of Georgian style homes. Federal homes often have two full stories plus a shorter attic story, in addition to the roof structure, making the entire building very tall. Brick is the most common exterior building material for Federal style homes and stone quoins are frequently utilized to distinctly mark the corners. A decorative balustrade often accentuates the very top of a hipped roof or surrounds the entire roof of the home, resting just above the eave. Decorative chimneys are slender, well defined and prominently displayed on the roof that is gabled or hipped with a very shallow pitch. The Federal-style front door is decorated with panels and is often covered by a small portico, supported by classically ordered columns or pilasters. The use of double-sash windows that begin at the floor and rise to the regular window height is a distinctly "Federal" feature.

FENESTRATION

Exterior openings for light and ventilation that penetrate the outside walls of a residence or building.

FINIAL

An ornamental design element atop a roof, gable, balustrade, turret, lantern, fence or post.

FIRE WALL

A non-combustible wall constructed between attached buildings or to separate sections of a structure to prevent the spread of fire.

FISH SCALED SHINGLES

Wooden shingles cut and lapped in a pattern resembling fish scales.

FIXED GLASS

An inoperable glass window that is stationary within its frame and cannot be opened.

FLAT-HEADED WINDOW

A window with a horizontal (square) top.

FLAT ROOF

A roof without slope or having only a slight pitch so as to drain away rainwater.

FLEMISH BOND

A pattern of brickwork where the exposed ends of the bricks (headers) alternate within each course with the exposed sides of the brick (stretchers). Every successive course of brick is staggered so that each header is carefully centered on the stretchers in the courses directly above and below it.

FLUTING

Parallel channels running vertically up the shaft of a column or pilaster in a closely spaced pattern.

FOUNDATION

The system of structural support between a principal building (superstructure) and the ground beneath. A building foundation serves to transmit loads from the superstructure directly to the earth below.

FOYER

The vestibule, entrance hall or transitional space from the exterior of a building to the interior spaces.

FRENCH ARCHITECTURE

The French style of architecture became popular in America after World War I when the American soldiers serving in France returned home with a familiarity and fondness for the French style of architecture. The French style in America is eclectic. Its precedents are rooted in French domestic architecture, specifically in the regions of Brittany and Normandy. The French style exhibits great variety in form, in the ornamentation and detailing, and in the use of materials. A massive, steep, hipped roof, often appointed with dormer windows, typically unites the French house. This style of architecture is often asymmetrical in form and occasionally includes a rounded tower element on the principal façade of the structure. Though informal in style, French houses can exhibit impressive Renaissance detailing.

FRENCH CHATEAUX

A monumental style of French architecture with opulent design details derived from the late Gothic style and Italian Renaissance styles. French Chateaux-style homes in America are often modeled after the chateaux of the Loire Valley as an extravagant display of personal wealth.

FRENCH COLONIAL ARCHITECTURE

Most of the surviving examples of original French Colonial architecture (1700-1830) are located in Louisiana, along the Mississippi River. The roof of a French colonial house often had double pitches. Since many of these homes had no hallways, there was often a wide gallery circumscribing the house. A large hipped roof was built to cover the main volume of the building that transitioned to a lower pitched roof extending over the gallery. Rural French colonial residential construction differs form its urban counterpart in that the main floor is usually built high above the ground on masonry foundations to protect the home from periodic flooding. Galleries usually surround the home with rows of thin wooden posts supporting the lower slope of the roof. Rural French colonial homes were generally much larger than city houses built in the same style. Porches and galleries were a very important feature of French Colonial homes and they distinguish this style from many others. French Colonial homes often consist of two stories. French colonial doors are divided in half vertically, creating two smaller, narrower doors within one frame. Like French doors, windows have the same vertical division and operate as casements rather than sliding up-and-down.

FRENCH DOORS

A pair of matching full-length doors operating within the same opening, each having a top rail, bottom rail, and stiles, with wood panels or glass panes at the top to bottom.

FRENCH NORMANDY

French Normandy homes were usually asymmetrical houses constructed of brick, stone, or stucco. The exterior walls are often fabricated to appear as if they were built using techniques known as bousillage and briquette-entre-poteaux. The exposed framing members are set in a geometric pattern of square and diagonal timbers, between which the triangular open spaces are filled with brick or stucco. The American adaptation of the rural farm houses of Normandy often features a cylindrical tower with a cone-shaped roof attached to the façade and forming the front entrance. Other typical features include a steeply pitched roof with dormers, flared eaves, casement windows, and one or more massive chimneys.

FRENCH PROVINCIAL

French Provincial architecture is generally asymmetrical in design and sometimes features a cylindrical tower on the façade. The mass of the French Provincial home is dominated by a steeply pitched, hipped roof. A distinctive design element of this style is the second story dormer window that breaks through the eave of the roof, with the face of the dormer becoming a vertical extension of the façade wall below. These windows are usually arched at the top and provide light and ventilation in the attic rooms. American homes classified as French Provincial or French Country are usually an eclectic combination of the rural design elements borrowed from the French countryside.

FRENCH WINDOWS

A long pair of casement windows extending to floor level and mounted within the same opening that are hinged to open in two leaves similar to a pair of doors.

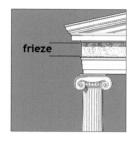

FRIEZE

The middle section of a classical entablature situated between the architrave and cornice. This continuous horizontal band is often decorated with sculpture in low relief. Also an exterior eave line or horizontal band at the top of a wall, immediately below the ceiling plane.

FRONT ELEVATION

The façade or principal face of a building or residence.

G

GABLE

The triangular wall segment at the end of a pitched roof above the level of the eaves. The edges of the triangular gable walls meet the sloping ends of the roof. The bottom of the gable is defined by a horizontal line extending between the eaves on opposite sides of the roof. A stepped gable has stepped parapet walls at the ends of the roof. A Dutch gable has curved parapet walls at the ends of the roof. A hipped gable slopes back at the uppermost part.

GABLED ROOF

A sloped or pitched roof with triangular wall segments above the eaves at one or both ends.

GALLERIED HOUSE

A dwelling that has one or more covered porches on the exterior of the structure.

GALLERY

A long covered porch on the exterior of a building or a long covered area serving as a corridor within a building. Also a space utilized for the display of artwork.

GAMBREL ROOF

A ridged roof that has two pitches on each side with the lower slope being steeper than the gently sloping upper section of the roof.

GAZEBO
A small detached decorative or ornamental structure in the form of a pavilion providing shelter or serving as an observation point in a park, garden or outdoor area.

GEORGIAN ARCHITECTURE
Georgian architecture was the dominant style of houses in the English colonies from 1700 to 1780. Simple elegance and formality were the essence of the Georgian style, as were the principles of geometric proportion and symmetry. Windows of a Georgian house are always evenly spaced and in alignment horizontally and vertically on the principal elevations. The front door is typically centered on the façade of the house and is always accented with decorative architectural elements, such as a pediment or curved hood supported by small columns or pilasters. Georgian-style residences are generally constructed with two stories above ground level and a tall, high-pitched roof set above the main structure. Georgian façades are almost always perfectly symmetrical. A cornice with decorative moldings or dentils is situated below the eave to embellish the

façade at the soffit. Ornamentation on Georgian-style homes is usually restricted to the decorative features surrounding the doors and windows. The Georgian roof is often appointed with dormer windows.

GEORGIAN ARCHITECTURE – MIDDLE ATLANTIC
In the middle Atlantic colonies, brick or stone was the most common building material used to construct Georgian style homes. Georgian home in the middle-Atlantic colonies typically have heavier moldings and details. Gabled roofs are common and cornices below the roof are often decorated with modillions or dentil work. Windows are double-hung and usually contained six glass panes in the upper sash and a matching lower sash. However, these double-hung windows sometimes had sashes with six, nine or twelve window panes.

GEORGIAN ARCHITECTURE – NEW ENGLAND
Gable and gambrel roofs commonly appear on wood-framed Georgian style homes with clapboard siding constructed in the New England region.

Georgian houses in New England usually have paneled front doors flanked by classically ordered pilasters supporting a pedimented entablature. The transom window above the entrance door is either semi-circular or rectangular in shape. Upper floor windows are placed just below a classically proportioned cornice, set directly below the eave and usually decorated with modillions on the soffit. Windows on the lower floor correspond in size to the upper story. A balustrade set on the roof is another identifying feature of the Georgian style in New England.

GEORGIAN ARCHITECTURE IN THE SOUTH
Brick was the most common material used to construct Georgian homes in the southern colonies and exterior brickwork was laid in Flemish bond. Roofs on southern Georgian houses are hipped and window panes are generally small. The cornice below the eave is always classically proportioned and detailed with modillions. A pedimented doorway at the center of the façade occasionally features a rectangular or semi-circular transom window. Variations of these design features appear on the same basic building type for all Georgian architecture, regardless of the geographic region.

GINGERBREAD
Exterior ornamental woodwork in the form of spindlework, scrollwork, decorative brackets, pendants, and jigsaw designs cut into wooden bargeboards.

GOTHIC ARCH
A pointed arch with both sides curving downward from the apex to a horizontal sill or floor plane.

GOTHIC ARCHITECTURE

The Gothic style was characterized by pointed arches, rib vaults, flying buttresses, delicate arcades, and large clerestory windows. The style emerged during the Middle Ages in Europe following the Romanesque and Byzantine periods. Gothic architecture featured a dramatic reduction of massive walls and introduced a system of large, tall and richly decorated windows. Special features include height and brightness created by the skeletal structure and windows of a stained glass. Notre Dame in Paris is an example of the Gothic style.

GOTHIC REVIVAL

A romantic architectural style distinguished by vertically pointed arches, steeply pitched gable roofs, finials and medieval decorative motifs. Gothic Revival residences featured wide verandas and octagonal towers or turrets. An example of the Gothic Revival style is the Houses of Parliament in London.

GRADE

The ground level at the perimeter of a building.

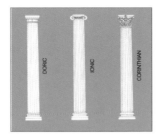

GREEK COLUMNS

Bold columns based upon the classical orders of ancient Greek architecture.

GREEK REVIVAL

This Neoclassical architectural style is based upon the simplicity of structure and form of ancient Greek buildings. Buildings of this style are either square or rectangular in plan with classical proportions. Facades are symmetrical and silhouettes are bold. Greek Revival residences have bold proportions and large classical columns or pilasters beside the front entry portal that often features a shallow pediment.

GREEK REVIVAL PLANTATION

The classical proportions and traditional architectural components of the Greek Revival style strongly influenced the design of plantations built in the South in the early to mid-1800s before the Civil War. The Greek Revival façade is always symmetrically arranged and the window's are evenly spaced. A belvedere or widow's walk is frequently placed at the peak of the roof structure. The most prominent architectural element is the row of giant, two-story columns covering the façade of the structure and supporting a broadly overhanging roof to create a wide front gallery. Greek Revival plantation homes are commonly painted white, or another light color, and the exterior columns are always designed and scaled according to ancient Greek rules of proportion. The main entrance is more elaborately decorated than other parts of the façade and often includes glass sidelights and an elliptical or rectangular transom above the door. On the interior, a grand staircase frequently appears in the foyer, elegantly situated near a large formal ballroom on the main floor. Windows were usually short, double-hung openings on the ground floor with taller, rectangular shaped windows on the second floor. The main entrance to the Greek Revival plantation home was at the ground floor level. Greek Revival doors were typically solid wood.

GREEK RULES OF PROPORTION

The mathematical guidelines for scale and proportion of architectural elements established by ancient Greek designs.

GRILLE

An ornamental arrangement of metal, wood or stone bars forming a screen to cover and protect an opening.

GROIN VAULT

A compound vault comprised of two barrel vaults intersecting at right angles. When applied to a ceiling, the intersecting barrel vaults form arched walls or openings below on each of the four sides of the covered area.

HIPPED ROOF
The sloping ridge of a roof formed at the intersection of two adjoining roof surfaces pitched in different directions. The eaves of a hipped roof are horizontal at the perimeter without gables ends.

IONIC ORDER
A classical Greek Order characterized by slender columns that are usually fluted and have scroll-like volutes featured on the capital.

ITALIAN ARCHITECTURE
Italian architecture became a prevalent style in America shortly before the Civil War. It was very popular in areas that experienced significant growth in the United States during the mid-to-late 1800s. Italian architecture has evolved more recently to the simplicity and elegance of contemporary revivals of classical styles. Italian architecture has retained a distinct appearance that is easily identifiable when compared with other styles. Architectural design elements, such as the campanile and belvedere or even a heavily bracketed cornice, are very distinctly Italian architectural features. The Italian style of architecture is usually classified in three categories: Italian Renaissance Revival, Italianate, and Italian Villa. Italian architecture typically includes the use of a thick, heavy cornice with brackets or dentils, a low-pitched or flat roof, restrained and dignified ornamentation, and a simple building material such as stone masonry or scored stucco.

HALF-TIMBERING
Exposed timber-framed structural members that remain visible after infilling between support and bracing members with plaster, nogging, wattle, daub, or brick.

HOOD
A projection above a window, door or exterior opening to provide protection from the weather.

IRONWORK
Structural or ornamental building components fabricated of cast iron, wrought iron or steel.

HIGH-PITCHED ROOF
A very steep roof.

ITALIAN RENAISSANCE REVIVAL ARCHITECTURE

The Italian Renaissance Revival style of architecture (1880-1920) features design characteristics influenced by the palaces built during the Renaissance period in Tuscany and northern Italy. Houses built in this style are highly symmetrical, very formal and typically feature a heavy cornice, decorated with dentils or modillions, wrapping around a freestanding building. The Italian Renaissance Revival style rarely made use of columns. Exterior ornamentation includes heavy rustication (stone blocks or scored stucco) on the ground floor, quoins (stacked corner blocks), and arched, hooded windows. This style of building was always constructed of stone or stuccoed brick. Italian Renaissance homes feature grand, exterior staircases leading to a prominent main floor. The main floor of the residence is typically situated at the second floor level. The first floor level is often partially submerged below grade. The Italian Renaissance roof structure is typically hipped, low-pitched and understated by comparison to the rest of the exterior design. The roof usually overhangs the building creating large eaves. A large and prominent entablature always appears on Italian Renaissance buildings, just below the eave. The main floor windows are taller, more decorative and ornate than windows on other levels.

ITALIAN VILLA ARCHITECTURE

Italian Villa style homes built in America (1845-1870) were designed to emulate manor houses of the Italian countryside. Although generally rambling and irregular in plan, they were cohesive in design and carefully confected to be more convenient for the occupants. The Italian Villa was typically an irregular, asymmetrically shaped residential structure with a tower, or campanile, on the principle façade that appears as the defining characteristic of this style. The tower was often placed off-center so as to enhance the asymmetric design of the façade. The lack of demand for symmetry in Italian Villa style allowed for a convenient plan with rooms and spaces that flowed into one another. The Italian Villa style is easily distinguished by the use of heavily ornate and decorative brackets on the cornices below the eaves of the roof.

The main structure is typically comprised of two stories with a tower that rises 1 to 1 1/2 additional floors. The Italian Villa roof is a low-pitched hipped structure with large, overhanging eaves. Like other Italian styles, Italian Villas have a thick band that runs horizontally around the building, just below the roof projection, called the entablature. Massive, heavily ornate brackets support the projecting eaves of the roof. A long, one-story porch typically runs across all or part of the principal façade or a veranda wraps around a portion of the Italian Villa-style residence. Windows are often tall, arched and commonly set in pairs or by three.

ITALIANATE ARCHITECTURE

The first Italianate-style homes in America were built in the early 1840s and this style dominated the design of American residences until 1890. These homes were similar to the houses built in the Italian Villa style, however, they did not feature a tower or campanile and were often less complex in detailing. Homes built in the Italianate style included a traditional low-pitched hipped roof that was often topped by a cupola or lantern, deep cornices with elaborately articulated brackets, and tall, narrow windows that were frequently curved or arched at the top. Italianate homes can be built of stone or brick masonry, wood, or even wood framing with a smooth stucco finish. Italianate homes frequently have small entry porches that only rise to the bottom of the second story. A very thick entablature is always included in the design of an Italianate building. This cornice and frieze are highly ornate and are decorated with large, elaborate brackets that support the broadly overhanging eave. Brackets adorning the entablature of an Italianate residence are always evenly spaced and can be placed individually or in pairs. Italianate homes are often box-shaped, having square plans typically consisting of two or three stories above the ground. Italianate-style homes often have arched windows with highly crafted and ornate hoods or crowns. All windows and doors are placed in a symmetrical arrangement about the principal façade. Windows are commonly arranged in pairs or even in sets of three.

JACK ARCH

A flat arch above a window or door comprised of splayed brickwork.

JAMB

The vertical sides of a window or door frame that are fastened to the wall, forming the opening to which a door or window sash is installed.

JIGSAW WORK
Curvilinear shapes of decorative wood-work made with a jigsaw.

JOISTS
A system of horizontal structural members spanning between walls to support a floor or ceiling.

KEYSTONE
A wedge-shaped block installed at the crown of a masonry arch that is often larger and more ornate than the other stones forming an arch.

LANTERN
A small turret or tower crowning a roof or dome that is usually circular or polygonal with windows for light and air.

LEADED GLASS
Small decorative shapes of beveled or stained glass that are fastened together with lead strips to form a window or door panel.

LEVEE
A linear, sloped earthen embankment constructed beside a body of water to prevent flooding.

LINTEL
A horizontal load-bearing stone or structural beam bridging an opening to support the wall above a door or window.

LOGGIA
A covered area for outdoor living, integrated into the structure of a building, having an open colonnade or arcade on at least one side.

LOUVERED PANEL

A door or window panel comprised of a series of overlapping slats, blades, boards or bent metal fins that are either fixed in place or adjustable. Louvered panels are designed to allow ventilation and light to penetrate while blocking rain and visibility.

LOUVERED SHUTTERS

Operable window or door panels comprised of a series of overlapping slats for ventilation, privacy and storm protection.

LOWER PITCHED ROOF

The more gently sloped section of a double-pitched roof having two different roof angles.

LOWER SASH

The movable bottom section of an operable double-hung window.

LOW-PITCHED ROOF

A roof plane with a very gentle slope where the vertical rise is significantly less than the horizontal run.

MANOR HOUSES

The country residence of the lord of a manor or the most important home in a village. In the later Middle Ages, manor houses were medium-sized, unfortified residences of the affluent. Imposing plantation homes in the southern United States are a form of manor houses.

MANSARD ROOF

A popular French style of roof, also known as a gambrel roof, having a very steeply pitched lower slope that is nearly vertical and can be slightly curved. The upper portion of the roof has a very low pitch that is almost horizontal.

MEDALLIONS

A decorative design element in bas-relief on an entablature or placed on a ceiling as ornamentation. Medallions are often cast in plaster and set at the center of a ceiling from which a chandelier is suspended.

MEDIEVAL

The architecture of the Middle Ages (400 A.D.-1400 A.D.) in Europe including Byzantine, Romanesque and Gothic periods. During the Middle Ages fortified castles were surrounded with small houses forming medieval towns. The medieval period ended with the Renaissance that spread throughout Europe in the 15th century.

MEDITERRANEAN STYLE

Mediterranean-style homes generally connote an Italian Renaissance residence located along the seacoast.

MILLWORK

Woodwork that is manufactured (dressed) at a mill with the use of mechanically driven rotary cutting tools.

MODILLIONS

A small, horizontal ornamental bracket, usually in the form of a scroll, used in a series to support the corona under the cornice of the Corinthian or Composite Orders.

MOLDING

A shaped band of wood or plaster with a decorative profile, either inset or projecting, such as door and window casings, baseboards, cornices and trim on cabinetry.

MORTAR JOINTS

The exposed masonry joints between bricks, stones or tiles laid on a floor, wall or terrace.

MORTISE AND TENON

A technique for joining two wooden members by fitting the projecting rectangular end of one member (tenon) securely into a corresponding square-cut cavity (mortise) in the other.

MULLION

A vertical member forming the frame between panes of glass or panels in a window or door.

MULTILIGHT

A door or window comprised of many panes of glass.

MUNTINS

The wood or metal cross pieces or small bars that divide and support the panes of glass in a window or door.

NEOCLASSICAL STYLE

Architectural designs reflecting a return to classical forms and the principles of ancient Greek and Roman scale, proportions and ornamentation for buildings.

NEW ENGLAND STYLES

The architectural designs constructed by the pilgrims became the indigenous style of the New England region from 1600 through the mid-1700s. The Saltbox home and the Cape Cod cottage are two colonial styles that were built almost exclusively in New England. The Shingle style became popular in New England during the late 1800s. The Saltbox structure is typically 1 1/2 stories in front transitioning to only one story at the rear. From the ridge, the roof slants forward at a dramatic angle and has an elongated slope to the rear that resembles the shape of the old salt boxes made during the colonial period. The Cape Cod cottage is a very simple, rectangular structure comprised of one story with a steeply pitched roof that facilitates development of the attic cavity at the second floor level. The Cape Cod style is very simple and the room arrangement varies greatly in size and interior layout. Shingle-style homes are characteristically large and rambling houses. They are generally irregular in shape, vary in volume and often comprise an enormous structure. This distinctly American style acquired its name from the unique application of shingle material used as exterior siding.

NICHE

A shallow recess in a wall, often arched at the top and semicircular in plan, that is designed to contain a sculptural object or urn.

OPERABLE

A movable partition or element of fenestration (door or window) that can be opened or closed by sliding, swinging or lifting.

OPERABLE SASHE

Windows with two or more glass sections that slide or swing open or closed.

ORNAMENTATION

Decorative embellishment or details used to adorn the appearance of an architectural element, such as a column, pilaster, portico or façade.

OVERHANG

A roof projection above the face of the exterior wall or an upper story that projects beyond the enclosed area immediately below.

PAIRED WINDOWS

Two matching windows placed side by side and joined together to form a unit.

PALLADIAN WINDOW

A triple window comprised of a wide semi-circular central archway flanked by matching narrow, square-headed openings with flat entablatures. The arched window casing rests upon the entablatures of the adjacent rectangular side windows.

PALLADIO, ANDREA

An Italian architect of the Renaissance whose buildings inspired Neoclassical design in Europe.

PANELED DOOR

A door having one or more recessed panels set within a framework of rails, stiles and muntins.

PANES

Glass lights in a window sash subdivided by wooden cross pieces (muntins) or small bars.

PARAPET

The segment of an exterior masonry wall that extends above the roof line. A low protective wall along the edge of a roof or balcony.

PARTHENON

The temple of Athena (5th century B.C.) constructed in the Doric Order of classical architecture on the Acropolis in Athens.

PATTERN BOOK

A plan book featuring residential designs for new home construction and often facilitating the purchase of all required building components shipped to the building site.

PAVILION

A detached ornamental building or open structure used for entertainment or specialized activities, often located at the end of a visual axis.

PEAK FINIAL

An architectural ornament situated at the highest point on the roof.

PEDESTAL

The supporting block at the base of a column or statue.

PEDIMENT

A classical low-pitched triangular or segmentally curved gable above a façade, portico, doorway or window.

PEDIMENTED PORTICO

A classical façade element forming an entryway covered by a low-pitched triangular or segmentally curved gable.

PENDANT

An architectural ornament hanging or suspended from a ceiling or vault.

PERGOLA

A converted walkway feature in a garden comprised of an open gridded framework supported by a series of rhythmically or evenly spaced posts or columns and covered by trained vines or climbing plants.

PIER

A series of masonry supports used to elevate the floor level of a house building. The mass of solid masonry supporting an arch or occurring between doors, windows or other openings.

PILASTER

A pier or column that is attached (engaged) to the face of the wall, projecting slightly from the surface plane to reveal only a partial segment of the column including the base, shaft and capital.

PLASTER

A wall-finishing material composed of a mixture of lime or gypsum, sand and water to create a paste that is applied to a wall or ceiling in layers with a trowel producing a smooth finished surface when it hardens.

PIANO NOBILE

The main floor of an Italian palazzo (palace) that is raised one floor above ground level and contains the principal reception areas and entertaining rooms.

PIERCEWORK

Decorative perforations in a board used as ornamentation that are created by cutting openings in a flat wooded element.

PITCH

The slope of a roof defined as a ratio of the vertical height relative to a standard base dimension of twelve or the angle of the roof expressed in degrees.

PORCH

An exterior covered deck attached to a house or building having its own roof or incorporated into the structure and serving as a covered entryway.

PICTURE WINDOW

A large window comprised of a single fixed pane of glass overlooking a major exterior view.

PIGEONNIER

A one and one-half story structure with multiple openings in the exterior walls and interior niches for nesting doves or pigeons. The tower shaped outbuilding is usually square, octagonal, or circular in shape with a steep-pitched roof.

PITCHED GABLE

The flat triangular wall of a building situated between two steeply sloping roof planes above the eaves at the attic level.

PORTE-COCHÉRE

A covered porch forming an entrance through which vehicles can pass to facilitate passengers entering or departing under shelter.

PORTICO

An open or partially enclosed entrance porch projecting from the façade (antis) of a building or recessed into the structure (prostyle). The portico is usually positioned at the center of the façade and is often comprised of a series of columns or arches supporting a pediment.

POST

An upright or vertical structural member made of wood, stone or metal that is used to support part of a building.

POST AND BEAM

A structural framing system comprised of tall, thin vertical members (posts) supporting horizontal structural timbers (beams) that span between the upright supports (posts).

POST-MEDIEVAL ARCHITECTURE

Exposed timber-framed residential construction occurring between the Middle Ages in Europe and the Renaissance period. Steep roofs, small casement windows and large fireplaces are characteristics of this style.

PRINCIPAL FAÇADE

The front or main elevation of a building.

QUEEN ANNE STYLE

A style of architecture that evolved during the reign of Queen Anne in England (1702-1714) prior to the Georgian period.

QUOINS

A vertical series of brick, plaster, stone or wood blocks at the exterior corners of a building designed to visually or structurally enhance the exterior design.

RAFTER

One of a series of sloping structural framing members supporting a pitched roof.

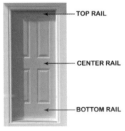

TOP RAIL

CENTER RAIL

BOTTOM RAIL

RAIL

Horizontal element of the frame of a door or window.

RAILING

A wood or metal member extending horizontally between two posts.

RAMBLING STYLE

An asymmetrical building layout or plan lacking in order and possibly having been developed over time in response to need without concern for comprehensive planning of the functional arrangement prior to construction.

RENAISSANCE DETAILING

Classical architecture appointments of the Renaissance period.

RENAISSANCE PERIOD

The span of time (1420-1550) during which the rebirth or reintroduction of classical architecture occurred in Europe.

RENAISSANCE STYLE

A style of architecture based upon the rebirth of classical Greek and Roman design principles that began in Italy (1420-1550) and spread throughout Europe. The Renaissance period replaced the Gothic style and influenced architectural design in Europe for several hundred years replacing Gothic spires with classical orders, motifs, semi-circular arches, symmetry and proportions.

RESTORATION

The process of returning an architectural edifice to the original condition when first constructed. This work often involves the removal of subsequent additions and modifications to the original structure, repair of architectural appointments, and replacement of missing elements or building components.

RIDGE

A horizontal roof line formed at the intersecting upper edges of two sloping roof planes.

ROMANESQUE REVIVAL STYLE

The Romanesque style of architecture (800 AD-1180 AD) is characterized by its use of the round arch and heavy masonry construction derived from Roman building types. Romanesque vaulted ceilings were semi-circular stone barrel shapes often with stone ribs. These ceilings were relatively low and massive in relation to towering Gothic structures. Ornamentation was sparse in Romanesque buildings that derived their decoration primarily from the structure.

ROOF PLANE

A surface of the roof that is uniformly sloped or flat and facing in one direction. The roof of a building may be comprised of more than one roof plane.

ROOF SPAN

The width of the open space created by structural supports for a roofing system. The width of the open space below a roof supported by beams, the length of a roof truss, or the width of an arched ceiling, vaulted ceiling or dome.

ROSETTE

A decorative architectural appointment or design element comprised of a round floral motif.

ROUND HEADED WINDOW

A type of window that is semi-circular, oval, elliptical or rounded at the top (head).

ROW HOUSES

A group of single family residences sharing common walls that are constructed on the adjoining property lines. Also known as townhomes or townhouses, these groups of dwellings often share uniform architectural design characteristics, appointments, plans and fenestration. Row houses are usually aligned to form a continuous façade along the street.

RUSTICATION

An architectural technique for creating the appearance of large stone block construction by cutting deep joints in masonry walls defining the desired pattern of stone wall composition. The surface texture of the stone blocks may be either rough or smooth depending upon the building design.

SALTBOX HOUSE

Saltbox-style homes (1600-1800) of the New England area are generally comprised of one and a half or two stories in height while the rear of the house is comprised of only a one story structure. This style of residential architecture is characterized by the irregularly shaped gabled roof that slants forward at a dramatic angle above the front of the house and has an elongated slope to the rear covering the one-story part of the structure. This distinctive feature originated by constructing a lean-to addition to the rear of a traditional colonial structure. The shape of the new structure resembled that of the saltboxes of the time. A centrally located chimney is a common element. In many Saltbox homes, the eave of the roof at the front of the structure overhangs the lower level by two or three feet. Decorative pendants adorn this overhang and the exterior surfaces where the gabled roof overhangs the facade. The original Saltbox homes of the 1600s had small diamond-shaped panes of glass installed in casement windows because larger panes were not available in the colonies.

SASH

The frame of a window into which the glass is set. Operable double-hung window sashes slide vertically, casement window sashes are hinged like doors, and other window sashes slide horizontally or are fixed in place and do not open.

SCROLL WORK

Any form of architectural ornamentation having the design motif of a scroll or scroll-like characteristics.

SCORED STUCCO

A masonry surface that is subdivided into a design pattern creating the appearance of stone blocks or bricks. See also rustication.

SEAMLESS
A material that continues without interruption of the surface texture.

SECOND EMPIRE
An eclectic French architectural style featuring a steeply pitched mansard roof creating a habitable upper story attic area nearly equal in size to the main floor. Other design elements include patterned slate roofing, shallow dormer windows, a tower or bay projecting from the center of the façade, and a heavy cornice with decorative brackets supportiong overhanging eaves.

SEGMENTED ARCH
The top of a window or door that is formed in the shape of a segment of a circle.

SHAKES
A hand-split siding or roofing material hewn from a short log in tapered pieces forming edge-grained shingles.

SHALLOW PITCH
A low-sloping surface commonly associated with a roof or porch deck.

SHED ROOF
A pitched roof that slopes in only one direction.

SHINGLE
A dimensional roofing material made of wood, asphalt, asbestos, slate, or metal that is installed in an overlapping pattern upon a sloped roof or exterior wall surface.

SHINGLE STYLE
Shingle-style homes are a unique regional type of American architecture that evolved mainly in New England along the northern Atlantic coast between 1874 and 1900. They feature the interesting use of wood shingles as exterior siding. Other characteristics of the Shingle style include large and prominent roof structures, wrapping verandas, turrets and towers. Wood shingles completely wrap the exterior walls of the Shingle style home and are placed continuously around the outer surface of the walls, even at the corners. Other exterior detailing is subdued so as to emphasize the shape of the shingle covered mass of the house. The roof of a Shingle-style home is typically very steeply pitched and irregular in shape so as to cover the irregular form of the structure. The roof is typically comprised of multiple levels that slope at various angles creating many different eave heights.

Towers are often placed on the facade of a Shingle-style home. A Shingle-style home may have as many as five or six different types of windows placed in an irregular pattern on the façade of the house. Arched windows are usually set in pairs or groups of three or four that are united by a continuous window frame. Small, rectangular windows are also commonly set in groups that are joined together side by side. The Shingle-style home often features a narrow, curving eyebrow window set on the roof.

SHUTTER
An operable window or door panel commonly installed in pairs on the exterior of a house or building for privacy or storm protection.

SIDELIGHTS
Fixed window(s) beside an entrance door that are relatively tall and narrow.

SIDING

An exterior surfacing material for buildings comprised of boards made of wood, metal, plastic or various composition materials that are laid in an overlapping horizontal pattern (clapboards), side-by-side vertically (board and batton), or notched together (tongue and groove).

SILL

The sloping horizontal member at the bottom of a door or window designed to prevent water intrusion. Also, the lowest horizontal structural member set above a masonry foundation to support a house or building.

SINGLE FAMILY HOME

A residence occupied by one family.

SLIDING WINDOW

An operable window comprised of one or more sliding sashes that open horizontally.

SLOPE

The pitch or angle at which a building component is set.

SOFFIT

The visible underside of an architectural element including the exposed surface below a roof overhang, entablature, arch, lintel or balcony.

SOUTHERN PLANTATION

The design of the Southern Plantation home (late 1700s - mid 1800s) often includes an arrangement of rooms around a central hall to allow for adequate air circulation. Deep, wrap-around porches were designed to shade the home from the harsh, southern heat and provide for outside living spaces that were protected from the rain. Plantation architecture was an eclectic blending of many different architectural concepts. These factors resulted in the development of a new style of large, stately homes that started to appear as the economy of the South began to flourish. Flood prone conditions made it necessary to raise the main floor. The ground floor of the plantation house was generally utilized for food preparation, storage and provided ancillary work areas for servants. The principle living areas of the Southern Plantation home were typically located on the higher level. Early Plantation homes are more basic and simple, while later examples became more refined and elaborate in their detailing. The grand appearance and ornate detailing of the Greek Revival plantations gave the impression that this was a period of great opulence. Other features contributing to the impressive appearance of these structures were massive porticos with multi-story columns, or a wide porch wrapping around the façade.

SPANISH COLONIAL ARCHITECTURE

Early houses built in the Spanish Colonial style (1600-1840) were simple by necessity because the regions where they were constructed were isolated and impoverished. Adobe brick or stone was used to construct the walls. Frequently the walls were heavily plastered, creating the unique massive curved profiles associated with this style. Spanish Colonial roofs were extremely low-pitched or completely flat and covered with layers of semi-cylindrical clay tiles. Bright colored paints are frequently used to adorn the façade and give life to the understated structure. Spanish Colonial homes often included a narrow porch that ran along the interior courtyard. These porches provided the only means of access to each room. The rambling forms of these homes were the result of constructing various rooms as needed. Spanish Colonial window openings consist of simple holes cut into the side of the house. Originally, no glass was used in the window opening. Wooden grilles often covered the windows to protect the interior from the elements. Spanish Colonial doors were crude holes cut into the exterior walls as a means of egress. Heavy wood shutters were placed on the exterior to close both windows and doors in the event of a storm.

SPANISH CONSOLE
An iron bracket projecting from a wall to provide structural support for a cantilevered gallery or balcony.

SPANISH STYLE
The Spanish constructed missions throughout the Southwest territory. These Spanish missionary churches inspired the Spanish Mission-style home. Spanish Colonial homes in the Southwest, Texas and Florida featured terracotta tile roofs, stucco walls, and detailed architectural ornamentation. Spanish Revival homes featured reference to their original European models including a stucco exterior, decorative wrought iron hardware, patterned tile and heavily carved columns and woodwork. In the early 1800s, the Spanish built ranches in California that became the model for suburban homes more than a century later. An Americanized version of the Spanish casa became known as the Monterey style. Dating from the early 1600s, the oldest house in America is a Pueblo-style residence for the Spanish governor built in Santa Fe.

SPINDLE
Long and narrow decorative wooden members turned on a lathe, such as the balusters on a staircase.

SPLIT SHINGLES
Wooden shakes.

SPRING POINT
The point at which the radius of an arch meets the straight vertical side of the supporting pier or column.

SQUARE-HEADED WINDOW
A window that is horizontal (flat) across the top (head).

STAINED GLASS
Colored glass material used to make decorative windows.

STEEP PITCH
Set at a steep incline, angle or slope.

STILE
The vertical framing millwork of a door or window sash to which the ends of horizontal rails are attached to fashion the framework.

STILTED ARCH
A segmental arch with its curvature raised by a short vertical extension (impost) of the pier or wall that commences above a horizontal band (string course) on the supporting structure.

STRAP HINGE
Long and narrow shaped operating hardware that is fastened horizontally to the face of a door, gate or shutter allowing it to swing open and closed.

STRING COURSE

A continuous horizontal band of masonry extending across the surface of an exterior wall, either flush or projecting with molded detail, marking the floor level of a building or structure.

STUCCO

An exterior plaster finishing material for buildings composed of a mixture of cement, lime, sand and water used to form flat surfaces, decorative moldings and relief work.

SURROUND

A decorative framework, trim or border around a window, door or portal.

SWAG

A form of classical festoon or ornamentation draped between two medallions or rosettes.

SYMMETRICAL

Identically corresponding forms matching in mirror-image on opposite sides of a central dividing line or axis.

SYMMETRY

Forms matching in mirror-image on opposite sides of a central dividing line or axis.

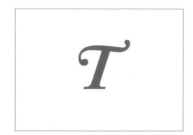

T

TERRA-COTTA TILE

A thin ceramic surfacing unit used for flooring, roofing and other building purposes produced with either a glazed or unglazed wearing surface.

THATCHED ROOF

A roof covered with straw or reeds fastened together to shed water and provide protection from the weather.

TIMBER FRAMING

A method of building construction employing heavy wooden timbers as the principle structural elements rising above the foundation to support the superstructure. Early timber-framed structures featured timber framing members connected by mortise and tenon joints fastened together with wooden pegs (trenals).

TOWER

A tall, vertical structure built of stone, brick or wood that is designed for viewing, defense or communication. Towers are generally round, square or polygonal. A belfry is a church tower and a campanile is a bell tower.

TOWNHOUSE

A row house that shares common (party) walls with the neighboring residences on either side. An urban dwelling comprised of one or more floors accommodating a single family. The façade is usually aligned with the front of the neighboring townhomes. Front yards, if any, are very shallow and no side yards are provided because the structures are abutting.

TRANSOM BAR

The fixed horizontal member of a door frame that separates the door from a panel, window or louvered vent above.

TRANSOM WINDOW

A smaller glazed opening of the same width placed directly above a door or window and separated by a horizontal bar.

TRIM

A decorative molding used to frame a door, window or cased opening or to edge a wall (baseboard) or ceiling, (crown molding) to cover joints and conceal seams between materials.

TRIM BOARD

A simple piece of finished material, usually having square edges, used to cover a joint, frame a door or window, serve as a baseboard, or edge a wall or ceiling to cover joints.

TRIPLE WINDOWS

A group of three windows that are mulled together into a single unit.

TRUSS

A triangular structural framing system comprised of a series of straight members arranged in smaller triangular patterns to create a rigid framework capable of spanning further than conventional beams.

TUDOR STYLE

A style of architecture that evolved in England in the late fifteenth and first half of the sixteenth century that included the reign of Henry VII and was named for his family (Tudor). The most prominent characteristic of the Tudor style is the exposed timber wall framing infilled with stucco creating a dramatic contrast between the dark brown or black wooden members and the whitewashed exterior masonry walls.

TURNED WOOD

Cylindrical wooden elements shaped on a lathe into a decorative pattern such as a spindle or baluster for a stair railing.

TURRET

A small slender tower forming a circular or polygonal bay usually situated at the corner of a fortified structure or building and having a steep, pointed roof.

U

𝒱

UPPER SASH
The glazed top section of an operable double-hung window.

VENTILATION
The process of providing fresh air and removing stale air in a room or building.

VERANDA
A shaded porch that extends along one or more sides of the building at the ground level and is covered by a roof.

VICTORIAN GOTHIC
A style of British architecture during the reign of Queen Victoria utilizing decorative bands of colorful and textured materials to highlight design elements, arches and the exterior corners of buildings. Fenestration included openings with Gothic arches and straight heads (tops). Finish materials were frequently displayed in colorful geometric patterns of pressed brick work and terra-cotta tile featuring foliated designs.

VICTORIAN ROMANESQUE
A period of Victorian architecture employing semi-circular arches supported by stone columns and incorporating decorative brick work and terra-cotta tile surfaces. Colorful exterior designs included brick and stone window surrounds, belt courses, quoins and stone walls. Fenestration varied in size and shape.

VICTORIAN STYLE
The architectural style that emerged in England during the age of Queen Victoria (1837-1901). In America, the Victorian style followed the Federal and Greek Revival periods of architectural design.

VIEUX CARRE
Generally known as the French Quarter, this area encompassed the early settlement of New Orleans that was laid out in a grid of city blocks fronting on a bend in the Mississippi River.

VOLUTE
A spiral or scroll-like shape used as ornamentation on the column capital of the Ionic Order or the spiraling end of a handrail above a newel post.

W

WEATHERBOARDS
Beveled siding consisting of long, narrow, overlapping boards applied horizontally to cover the exterior surface of a wood framed structure. Also known as clapboards.

WEST INDIES STYLE
West Indies-style plantations of the mid-to-late 1700s were large homes that were simple in detail and ornamentation. They were modeled after sugar plantations of the West Indies. The West Indies style features rounded posts that support the main floor gallery. Smaller columns that rest upon them support the gallery roof. The exaggerated scale of the support columns gives the upper story a taller and more elegant appearance. The West Indies style in America was also influenced by certain elements of the Acadian style. This style predates

the immense structures of the Greek and Classical Revival. The main floor of the West Indies-style plantation was usually built of wood framing. The lower or ground floor level was always constructed of hand made brick or heavy stone. Columns on the ground floor are generally shorter and thicker than the supports on the second floor that are more slender and elegant. Deep galleries surround the entire West Indies-style plantation structure that is covered by a massive, high-pitched roof. Dormer windows were commonly used.

WIDOW'S WALK
An observation platform with a perimeter railing set above the roof of a waterfront home.

WOOD CASING
The exposed molding around a door or window consisting of either flat or molded trim. Finished millwork surrounding any opening or used to cover a post, beam or structural member.

WOOD FRAMING
A structural system of wood construction supporting the walls, floors and roof of a building comprised of an assembly of studs, joists and rafters designed to carry lighter loads than heavy timber construction.

WOOD SHINGLES
Wooden roofing or siding material cut to uniform thickness and standard dimensions and installed in an overlapping pattern to cover the exterior surface of a sloping roof or face of a wall.

WOOD SIDING
Wood sheathing material laid either horizontally or vertically depending upon exposure to weather to cover an interior or exterior surface of a building. Siding may be installed with overlapping joints, rabbited joints, tongue and groove joints, board and baton joints, or butt jointed.

WOODEN TRIM
Casing materials and moldings made of wood that are used to cover joints in materials, create door and window surrounds, baseboards, cornices and other finished woodwork.

WOODWORK
Building elements fabricated from wood and installed as parts of a structure including casework, trim, panels, moldings, railings and cabinetry.

WRAP-AROUND PORCH
A veranda, gallery or covered exterior terrace extending continuously around one or more corners of a structure.

Bibliography

COLONIAL

Garrett, Wendell. American Colonial: Puritan Simplicity to Georgian Grace. New York: Monacelli Press, Inc., 1995.

Howells, John Mead. Lost Examples of Colonial Architecture: Buildings That Have Disappeared or Been So Altered as to be Denatured. New York: Dover Publications, Inc., 1963.

David Larkin, et al. Colonial: Design in the New World. New York: Stewart, Tabori and Chang, Inc., 1988.

CONTEMPORARY

Wagner, Walter F. Jr. A Treasury of Contemporary Houses. New York: McGraw Hill, Inc., 1978.

Wallace, Phillip B. Colonial Houses. New York: Bonanza Books, 1931.

FEDERAL

Beard, Geoffrey. The Work of Robert Adam. London: Bloomsbury Books, 1978.

Bolton, Arthur T. The Architecture of Robert and James Adam - Volume I. England: Country Life Ltd., 1922.

Bolton, Arthur T. The Architecture of Robert and James Adam - Volume II. England: Country Life Ltd., 1922.

Garrett, Wendell. Classic America: The Federal Style and Beyond. New York: Universe Publishing, 1995.

Hibbert, Christopher. Chateaux of the Loire. Japan: Alvin Garfin, 1982.

Parissien, Steven. Adam Style. London: Phaidon Press Limited, 1992.

FRENCH

Bernard, Catherine and Marlene Gsell. The French Riviera. Paris: Herme-Paris, 1998.

Buchholz, Barbara and Lisa Skolnik. French Country. New York: Friedman/Fairfax Publications, 2000.

Faucon, Régis and Yves Lescroart. Manor Houses in Normandy. Paris: Könemann, 1977.

Gebelin, François. The Chateaux of France. France: Ernest Benn Limited and G. P. Putnam's Sons, 1964.

Melot, Michel. Chateaux of the Loire. Köln: Evergreen, 1997.

Miquel, Pierre, Jean Baptiste Leroux. The Chateaux of the Loire. Hachette-Livre: Les Editions Du Chene-Hach, 1998.

Phillips, Betty Lou. French by Design. Salt Lake City: Gibbs Smith, Publisher, 2000.

Phillips, Betty Lou. French Influences. Salt Lake City: Gibbs Smith, Publisher, 2001.

Pozzoli, Milena Ercole. Châteaux of the Loire: Places and History. Paris: Librairie Gründ, 1996.

Slesin, Susan and Cliff Stafford. French Style. New York: Clarkson N. Potter, Inc., 1984.

GENERAL

Baker, John Milnes. American House Styles: A Concise Guide. New York: W.W. Norton and Company, 1994.

Ballinger, Richard M. and Herman York. The Illustrated Guide to the House of America: A Region by Region Survey of Contemporary and Traditional Residential Houses. New York: Galahad Books, 1971.

Bolton, Arthur T. Architecture of Robert and James Adam, Vol. 1. Woodbridge: Baron Publishing, 1984.

Bolton, Arthur T. Architecture of Robert and James Adam, Vol. 2. Woodbridge: Baron Publishing, 1984.

Daley, Sue and Steve Gross. Santa Fe Houses and Gardens. New York: Rizzoli International, 2002.

Dennis, Landt. Behind Adobe Walls. San Francisco: Chronicle Books, 1997.

Fletcher, Sire Bannister. A History of Architecture. Boston: Architectural Press, 1996.

Hamlin, Talbot Faulkner. The American Spirit in Architecture. New Haven: Yale University Press, 1926.

Kemp, Jim. American Vernacular: Regional Influences in Architecture and Interior Design. New York: Viking Penguin, Inc., 1987.

Klein, Marilyn W. and David P. Fogle. Clues to American Architecture. Washington, D.C.: Starrhill Press, 1995.

Massey, James C. and Shirley Maxwell. House Styles in America: The Old-House Journal Guide to the Architecture of American Homes. New York: Penguin Group, 1996.

Mather, Christine and Sharon Woods. Santa Fe Style. New York: Rizzoli International, 1986.

McAlester, Virginia and Lee. A Field Guide to American Houses. New York: Alfred A. Knopf, Inc., 1984.

McAlester, Virginia and Lee. Great American Houses. New York: Abbeville Press, 1994.

Moore, Suzi. Under the Sun-Desert Style and Architecture. Boston: Bulfinch Press, 1995.

Norbeg-Schulz, Christian. Meaning in Western Architecture. New York: Rizzoli International Publications, Inc., 1980.

Rifkind, Carole. A Field Guide to Contemporary American Architecture. New York: Penguin Group, 1998.

Riseboro, Bill. The Story of Western Architecture. New York: Charles Scribner's Sons, 1979.

Salny, Stephen M. Country Houses of David Adler. New York, W. W Norton and Company, 2001.

Smith, George Everard Kidder. A Pictorial History of Architecture in America. New York: American Heritage Publishing Co., Inc., 1976.

Wilson, Chris and Robert Reck. Facing Southwest. New York: W. W Norton and Company, 2001.

GEORGIAN

Cranfield, Ingrid. Georgian House Style: An Architectural and Interior Design Source Book. Cincinnati: F and W Publications, Inc., 2001.

Parissien, Steven. The Georgian House: in Britain and America. New York: Rizzoli International Publications, Inc., 1995.

Spencer-Churchill, Henrietta. Classic Georgian Style. New York: Rizzoli International Publications, Inc., 1997.

ITALIAN

Black, Alexandra. Tuscan Elements. New York: Watson Guptill, 2002.

Clark, Jane Gordon. Italian Style. Holbrook: Adams Media Corporation, 1999.

Fairweather, Catherine. La Dolce Vita. Boston: Bulfinch Press, 2001.

Howard, Edmund. Italia, The Art of Living Italian Style. New York: St. Martins Press, 1997.

Stoeltie, Barbara and Rene. Country Houses of Tuscany. Köln: Taschen, 2000.

Toledano, Ralph. Italian Splendor. New York: Universe Publishing, 1995.

NEW ENGLAND

Doane, Doris. A Book of Cape Cod Houses. Boston: David R. Godine, 2000.

Mallary, Peter T. Houses of New England. New York: Thames and Hudson, 1984.

Meisel, Susan and Ellen Harris. The Hamptons. New York: Harry N. Abrams, Inc., 2000.

Schuler, Stanley. The Cape Cod House: America's Most Popular Home. Exton: Schiffer Publishing, Ltd., 1982.

Roth, Leland M. Shingle Styles-Innovation and Tradition in American Architecture. New York: Harry N. Abrams, Inc., Publishing, 1999.

Schuler, Stanley. Saltbox and Cape Cod Houses. Atglen: Schiffer Publishing, Ltd., 2000.

SPANISH

Junquera y Mato, Jaun Jose. Spanish Splendor. New York: Rizzoli International, 1992.

SOUTHERN PLANTATION

Cooper, J. Wesley. Antebellum Houses of Natchez. Natches: Southern Historical Publications, 1970.

Gleason, David King. Plantation Homes of Louisiana and the Natchez Area. Baton Rouge: LSU Press, 1982.

Gleason, David King. Great Houses of Natchez. Jackson: University Press of Mississippi, 1986.

Gleason, David King. Antebellum Homes of Georgia. Baton Rouge: LSU Press, 1987.

Gleason, David King. Virginia Plantation Homes. Baton Rouge: LSU Press, 1989.

Stahls, Paul F., Jr. Plantation Homes of the Teche Country. Gretna: Pelican Publishing Company, 1992.

Acknowledgments

The majority of new homes appearing in *Creating Your Architectural Style* were designed by The Hopkins Company, AIA. We deeply appreciate the confidence of our clients who awarded the responsibility for designing their homes to our architectural firm. Their friendship and gracious hospitality in allowing us to photograph these homes contributed immeasurably to the content of *Creating Your Architectural Style*.

Four key members of our staff have worked together collectively designing the residences featured in *Creating Your Architectural Style* with the combined effort totaling more than one hundred years – George D. Hopkins, Jr., Janis Z. DeVidts, Steven R. Quarls and Eric M. Grieshaber. As a team, we developed the design concepts, plans and specifications for each home and managed the office.

Digital renderings and photographic layouts included in *Creating Your Architectural Style* were prepared and assembled by Janis Z. DeVidts. Many of the watercolor renderings are works by Jim Blanchard, artist. The graphic design of this book was developed by George Hopkins, Janis DeVidts, Jedd Haas of EPS, Inc. and Scott Ott of Scott Ott Creative, Inc.

My special thanks to Dr. S. Frederick Starr for encouragement, advice regarding the approach to publication and writing the Foreword. Neale Sweet provided valuable insights from an outstanding career in publishing. Mikko Macchione edited the copy that was refined with the assistance of Janis DeVidts and the watchful eye of Jedd Haas.

My wife, Deborah Hopkins, contributed her appellate legal skills in proofreading the manuscript – an offer I should have accepted for my dissertation at Tulane.